Hendrik Frensen Verwoerd South Africa's Greatest Prime Minister

Stephen Mitford Goodson

Hendrik Frensch Verwoerd South Africa's Greatest Prime Minister
Stephen Mitford Goodson
First edition July 2016
Second edition April 2017

Copyright © 2016 Stephen Mitford Goodson

All rights reserved. No part of this book maybe reproduced in any form by any electronic or mechanical means including photocopying, recording, or information storage and retrieval without permission in writing from the author.

ISBN Number
1717041426

Dedication

This book is dedicated to the memory of S E D Brown, editor of *The South African Observer* (1955-1990) and one of South Africa's foremost political thinkers.

"In a multi-racial society where power must eventually be transferred into the hands of the numerically stronger Bantu, not only the White, but also the Coloured and Indian will go under. Over time even the Bantu masses will not benefit because on the strength of what has happened elsewhere in Africa, it must be taken into consideration that South Africa will develop into an autocracy or dictatorship. On account of their lack of ability to manage a complicated administration, the country will moreover administratively and economically be destroyed[1] and for everyone – White and Coloured – end in chaos" – Dr. H. F. Verwoerd[2]

"We believe and trust in White leadership only. We believe in just racial apartheid. We believe in tutelage and apartheid. These three things are the source of our well-being and prosperity" – Richard Gert Forster, Chief of the 35,000 strong Griquas.[3]

By the Same Author

An Illustrated Guide to Adolf Hitler and the Third Reich
General Jan Christian Smuts The Debunking of a Myth
A History of Central Banking and the Enslavement of Mankind
Inside the South African Reserve Bank Its Origins and Secrets Exposed
Rhodesian Prime Minister Ian Smith The Debunking of a Myth
The Genocide of the Boers

Contents

Foreward 7

Introduction 12

Chapter

I   Youth 13

II   Academia 15

III   Editor of Die Transvaler 19

IV   Minister of Bantu Affairs (1950-1958) 22

V   Prime Minister (1958-1966) 37

VI   International Money Power 72

VII   Some General Observations 83

VIII   Assassination 88

IX   Conclusion 108

Maps 114

Appendix I 115
(Letter from Dr. H.F. Verwoerd to the author's
grandfather, Mr. S.M. Goodson.)

Appendix II 116
(Dr. H.F. Verwoerd's Notes for his speech of
6 September 1966.)

Appendix III 118
(Letter from the leader of the Herstigte Nasionale
Party, Mr. Jaap Marais, to the author.)

Reviews 119

Bibliography 133

Index 136

Foreword

A monograph on one of South Africa's most remarkable statesmen, Hendrik Frensch Verwoerd, who was murdered exactly 50 years ago when at the pinnacle of his brilliant term of office as Prime Minister of the Republic of South Africa, has appeared out of the pen of Stephen Goodson, well known expelled insider of the Reserve Bank of South Africa. In this Foreword Marthinus van Bart, specialist writer and cultural journalist of 40 years standing, discusses Verwoerd and the biography *Hendrik Frensch Verwoerd: South Africa's Greatest Prime Minister*.

When evaluating Hendrik Frensch Verwoerd (1901-1966) as one of the greatest statesmen of the modern world, one cannot, first of all, overlook the stature of another Afrikaner statesman and predecessor of 80 years earlier whose divine mantle as real leader of his people fell on Verwoerd's shoulders. This man was President Stephanus Johannes Paulus Kruger. Kruger was four times elected President of the Zuid-Afrikaansche Republiek (ZAR) "and the man who was during his twenty years of office the most conspicuous figure in the history of South Africa".[i] Like Kruger, Verwoerd was for the eight years of his leadership in the spotlight on the World's political stage, and "his life and his acts may be said to have constituted the history of South Africa".[ii] In his biography on Kruger - first published in 1941: *Paul Kruger - His Life and Times*[iii] Judge Manfred Nathan states: "Many have spoken of Cecil Rhodes [most visible figurehead of the powerful Anglo American hegemony] as the rival and antagonist of Kruger. This, however, was merely accidental. Had Rhodes not been there, Kruger would still have played a great and, in some respects, a commanding part in South African affairs".[iv]

"The struggle of Paul Kruger to maintain independence [for the ZAR], although from the point of view of visible success it failed in the end, was not unavailing. Amid the distractions of a divided people, poor and almost entirely lacking material resources, he welded apparently conflicting elements into one cohesive whole. Though at first ill-supported by those who should have sustained him in his efforts, he converted a disunited and enfeebled community into one that was united and self-reliant. At the beginning he was derided and distrusted, while those who were opposed to him on national and racial grounds lost no opportunity of denigrating his efforts

---

[i]   Judge Manfred Nathan, *Paul Kruger - His Life and Times*, The Knox Publishing Company, Durban, 1944, p. 1
[ii] Judge Manfred Nathan, *Paul Kruger - His Life and Times*, p. 1
[iii] Judge Manfred Nathan, *Paul Kruger - His Life and Times*, The Knox Publishing Company, Durban, 1944
[iv] Judge Manfred Nathan, *Paul Kruger - His Life and Times*, p. 1

and subjecting him to scorn and contempt, not unmixed with hate; but he triumphed over these things, and if not during his life, then certainly after his death his opponents and his enemies paid involuntary tribute to the great qualities which were his".[v]

Nathan equals Kruger to the American statesman, Abraham Lincoln, "who liberated the slaves from bondage and his own people from narrowness of spirit into a wider conception of justice and humanity. Kruger liberated his own equals; he taught them national self-reliance and self-respect. He showed them how to maintain the spirit of love for their own country, and justice to their fellow men. His example has been a lasting influence. He remained the founder of the South African spirit. He gave his people a soul."

The judge also states that Kruger's sincerity "caused men to feel that he was the father of his people, and that he was one who deserved and possessed the devotion as well as the respect due to a father. Yet, he was more than a *pater patriae*. He was the dominant figure. He not only wielded the fortunes of his country by dint of his own strong and unshakeable will, but, whether for good or ill, he influenced and perplexed and distracted the leaders of public opinion in Great Britain, that Power to whom he was for so many years opposed. If he aroused the bitterest antagonism of some among them, he caused these, as well as those who were well-disposed to him, to reflect, and sometimes even to change their policy with regard to South African affairs. In so doing, he drew upon himself the attention of the whole world. Such a man cannot be said to have been insignificant."

The judge concludes that Kruger "was not only the most conspicuous figure of his age. To men of future times, he remains a lasting influence. It may still be written that no one has had a greater power and stimulus than he upon the minds of his people for generations yet to come. He was a man of the people, he grew up with the people; he lived for the people."[vi]

Stephen Goodson in his well researched synoptic biography on Verwoerd analyses step by step the remarkable career of this brilliant man - spanning from an academic scholar and Professor of Sociology, Social Welfare, Psychology and Psycho technique to a pragmatic politician intent on rebuilding an Empire-ruined South African Union into a self-respecting, independent Republic of South Africa, a leader in World affairs and a home to all its inhabitants without striking out any community's individual culture and identity, leaving the self-image and self-respect of each intact.

---

[v]   Judge Manfred Nathan, *Paul Kruger - His Life and Times*, pp. 1-3
[vi]   Judge Manfred Nathan, *Paul Kruger - His Life and Times*, p. 478 (quoting J.F. van Oordt - D'Arbez)

On 2 September 1958 Dr. Hendrik Frensch Verwoerd (1901-1966) became the leader of the National Party - and with that appointment the sixth Prime Minister of the Union of South Africa. By his efforts, and amid great opposition, on 31 May 1961 South Africa became the Republic of South Africa. So modest was he, that he preferred that another, C.R. (Blackie) Swart, would be the first president of South Africa, and he himself remained Prime Minister.

Where Kruger left off in 1899, Verwoerd extended and enlarged all these virtuous deeds attributed to Kruger to do the same and much, much more for his people, all South Africans: the Afrikaner community, the English community, the diverse communities of European descent, as well as the coloured peoples and the diverse black peoples within our borders. He was a champion for all South Africa as a great country with a great nation, walking tall amongst the top nations and great countries of the world.

In his biography Judge Nathan revealed that Paul Kruger was proposed as the very first candidate for the Nobel Peace Prize of 1899, when it was established. Nominations for the award were considered by the Swedish Parliament in so far as it affected Science and Literature, and by the Norwegian Parliament in so far as it affected the Peace aspect. The proposal for Kruger was made by the member for Uppsala, and it was seconded by the member for Jönköping. A committee of five was appointed to report. At The Hague Peace Conference of 1899, it was decided not to award the prize to the heads of states.[vii] The first Nobel Peace Prize was only awarded in 1901 - to a British subject.

After Britain signed the Hague Treaty for Civilized Warfare in 1899 at this very conference - neither the Republic of Transvaal (Zuid-Afrikaansche Republiek) nor the Republic of the Orange Free State was invited - Britain proceeded to make war on the civilian inhabitants of the Boer Republics by means of scorched earth warfare. This rapine war was to enable the Empire to lay hold on the massive Witwatersrand gold reserves, coal and the rest of the mineral wealth of the country. As Kruger, the most excellent proponent for the Nobel Peace Prize in his time was Hendrik Verwoerd. But instead his life - and with that a civilized South Africa - was robbed from him by the deadly knife of a psychiatrically conditioned assassin of the international underworld money-and-power mafia. Instead, the Nobel Prize went to the two main icons of the dramatic demise of a once prosperous Republic, Nelson Mandela, who was convicted of terrorism and high treason, and his friend and equal, FW de Klerk, the last white president of the country. They were the combined recipients of the Nobel Peace Prize of 1993 awarded for "the peaceful demise of Apartheid".

[vii]   Judge Manfred Nathan, *Paul Kruger - His Life and Times*, Preface to the Fourth Edition, 1944

In 2001 de Klerk's wife, Marike, was brutally murdered in her secured home by an assassin. This was shortly after De Klerk deserted her in a scandalous adultery with the wife of a Greek shipping magnate.

Stephen Goodson's biography of 145 pages contains a reader-friendly and updated synopsis of Verwoerd's life and career. Then it zooms in on the enemies of Verwoerd and the motives for his assassination. Very interesting is the detailed reference to the secret Hoek Report of 1965 on the incredible wealth and power of the Anglo American Corporation (AAC) and its diverse affiliates, its links to international banking and governance, and the near absolute stranglehold it has on the South African financial world, as well as on the community at large. The title of the report, delivered in Afrikaans, is: *Die oormatige konsentrasie van kapitaal, produksie en bemarking binne die Invloedsfeer van 'n enkelbeheergroep, sy mag om te kan bepaal waar 'n groot gedeelte van die beskikbare kapitaalsfondse van die private sektor belê sal word, en dus waar werkverskaffing sal wees en nie sal wees nie, en moontlike teenmaatreëls*. Translated into English it reads: The Excessive Concentration of Capital, Production, and Market within the Sphere of Influence of a Single Controlling Group, its Power to determine where a Large Portion of the Available Capital Funds of the Private Sector shall be invested and where the Provision of Work shall be, and Possible Counter Measures.

In 1964 Prof. Piet Hoek, Professor in Economics of the University of Pretoria and assistant manager of Iscor, privately visited Verwoerd at his office and told him of his concern about the absolute power and influence of the AAC and the danger it posed for the peace and prosperity of the Republic. He asked Verwoerd if he could compile a report on the AAC to be tabled in Parliament. Verwoerd answered that he would welcome such a report. As Prime Minister he could not request it, but if he received this report, he would table it in Parliament. However, before the Hoek-report could be tabled, the Prime Minister was assassinated. Subsequently Prof. Hoek handed the report to Advocate B.J. (John) Vorster, who succeeded Verwoerd as Prime Minister. Vorster's reaction was to declare the report top secret and to forbid the publication thereof. This report has never been published and its contents have ever since been kept secret from the very people directly affected in their livelihood and daily lives by this almighty organisation, namely the diverse Peoples of the Republic of South Africa.

In this respect Dr. Louis Bothma of Bloemfontein in his recently published book *Vang 'n Boer* [viii] has the following to say on Verwoerd, the money powers and the assassination-drama of 50 years ago: In 1966 Verwoerd went from strength to strength - also in economic terms. In 1960 - after the attack on the

---

[viii] L.J Bothma, *Vang 'n Boer: Die stryd tussen Boer en Ovambo*, Self-published, Langenhovenpark, 2015, pp. 216-8

Sharpeville police station and subsequent shooting incident - South Africa was on the verge of a collapse. In 1966 the economic growth rate was 6% and the inflation rate 2%. On 31 July 1966 the newspaper *Rand Daily Mail* (one of the staunchest opponents of the Verwoerd government and apartheid) wrote: Dr. Verwoerd has reached the peak of a remarkable career . . . the nation is suffering from a surfeit of prosperity. But Verwoerd was worried that too much of this prosperity was in the hands of a money power wanting to put the apartheid project off track because it blocked its opportunity to make money. Political-wise big business wanted an integrated South Africa, not a divided but ethnically shared country. Verwoerd was well aware of this opposition and was worried that influential groups such as Anglo American, busy diversifying from mining to manufacturing and finance, would ultimately dictate the economic course of the country and eventually also the politics of South Africa. He therefore welcomed the initiative of Prof. Piet Hoek in 1964 to investigate the Anglo American Group and place a report on his desk for a revelation in Parliament. This Hoek Report was never made public by Verwoerd's successor, John Vorster. The specific reference in the report to Counter Measures was something Anglo American's chairman, Harry Oppenheimer, would not have liked. Oppenheimer, who represented Kimberley from 1948 to 1957 as a member of the United Party in Parliament and spokesman for this party's economic, financial and constitutional affairs, was an outspoken opponent of Verwoerd's apartheid-concept.

Bothma writes that in 1966, at the pinnacle of his political career, Verwoerd (as Paul Kruger of the old Transvaal Boer-republic) broadly obstructed the path of his enemies, overseas as well as within our borders - even within his own party. Frustrated because they were not succeeding in any direction (economics, military, politics, justice and diplomacy), these enemies of South Africa focused their attacks on the person of Dr. Hendrik Verwoerd.

On 28 August 1966 The *Sunday Tribune* featured an earth shattering editorial on its front page: 'Verwoerd must go' plan – Cape Nats back Anton Rupert: The knives are out in the Nationalist Party. Dr. Verwoerd faces the most serious split his Party has known since it came to power in 1948 – and Dr. Verwoerd is the main target. Nationalist rebels would like to see Dr. Verwoerd replaced by Mr. Anton Rupert, the politically moderate tobacco tycoon who has found acceptability in international circles, as no Nationalist Party leader has yet done . . . Now there has been a carefully planned operation to isolate Dr. Verwoerd and force a showdown. "Verwoerd must go. Verwoerd is the main target. The knives are out. A carefully planned operation to isolate Verwoerd. Verwoerd must fall . . . " writes Bothma. On 6 September 1966 Dr. Verwoerd was murdered in his seat in the House of Assembly.

Introduction

Hendrik Frensch[4] Verwoerd was the dominant figure in South African politics during the latter half of the twentieth century. After decades of dilly-dallying and indecision he rose above his contemporaries to provide a policy, a solution and a vision which would enable all the peoples of South Africa to participate and share in the wealth and prosperity of the country on a permanent basis.

When addressing black people Dr. Verwoerd often alluded to the image of a piano,[5] explaining that if there was to be melodious music and a harmonious society, both the black notes and white notes, in other words both races, would have to co-operate in a symbiotic relationship.

Dr. Verwoerd stood for fairness and justice for all and for the gradual emancipation of the Black people at their own pace. Having established a moral foundation, he was convinced that political independence and economic interdependence could flourish side by side. He viewed separate development as a temporary phase, whose aim was neither to dominate nor to discriminate, and stated on numerous occasions that human dignity is achieved by coexistence and not by living together. He was an honourable man of deep sincerity, who once informed an interviewer, "I never have the nagging doubt of wondering whether perhaps I am wrong".[6]

There were many notable achievements during his eight years in office – the establishment of the Republic, reconciliation between Afrikaans and English-speakers, resolution of the South West Africa issue in South Africa's favour and an economy growing at 6% per annum spurred on by the greatest programme of social and economic upliftment ever undertaken in South Africa's history, which resulted in the construction of vast townships, hospitals, clinics, schools, universities and sports facilities for black people.

Dr. Verwoerd was an implacable foe of the International Money Power and wanted to achieve complete autarky[7] and independence for South Africa. And then disaster struck at 2.14 on the afternoon of Tuesday, 6 September 1966 when a knife was plunged into the heart of South Africa by a hired assassin of the international bankers.

---

4   Pronounced "Frens", which is the Friesian form of Frans. Dr. Verwoerd's mother came from Friesland.
5   F. Barnard, *13 Jaar In Die Skadu Van Dr H.F. Verwoerd*, Voortrekkerpers, Johannesburg, 1967, 46.
6   G. Allighan, *Verwoerd -The End*, Purnell & Sons (S.A.) (Pty.) Ltd, Johannesburg, 1961, xxiii.
7   J. A. Marais, *Die era van Verwoerd*, Aktuele Publikasies, Pretoria, 1992, 11.

Chapter I
YOUTH

Hendrik Frensch Verwoerd, son of Wilhelmus Johannes Verwoerd and Anje (née Strik) was born on 8 September 1901 at Jacob van Lennepkade, Oudekerk, Amsterdam. He had an elder brother Leendert, who later became a well known plant pathologist, and a younger sister Hendrika (Lucie). His father ran a grocer's shop. He was very sympathetic to the Boer cause and organised a collection of funds in his town district during the second Anglo-Boer War (1899-1902).[8] In 1903 the family emigrated to Cape Town. His father set up business as a building contractor and settled in Mortimer Street, Wynberg, Western Cape. Young Hendrik first attended the Lutheran Primary School in Waterloo Street from 1907-1911 and then went to Wynberg Boys Junior School,[9] where he joined his elder brother, Len, who was in Standard VI. Hendrik passed Standard III in 1912.

Hendrik Verwoerd (11) centre with his father, Wilhelmus and sister, Lucie (4). The photograph was taken at their home in Wynberg, Cape Town in 1912.

---

8   F. Barnard, *op.cit.*, 20.
9   D.H. Thomson, *The Story Of A School A Short History of the Wynberg Boys' High School*, Wynberg, Cape, 1961, 121.

At the end of that year Hendrik's father obtained an appointment as assistant evangelist at the Dutch Reformed Church in Bulawayo, Rhodesia. Hendrik was sent to Milton High School whose school motto is Κλείστε εσείς όπως και οι άνδρες (Acquit ye like men). He attended the school from 1913-1917. He was a gifted scholar, winning many prizes, including a prize for being the best pupil in English literature in all the schools of Rhodesia.[10] He was a leading member of the debating society and a keen sportsman, playing cricket, rugby and tennis. He captained the cricket team and played as wicket keeper.[11] In his last year he was awarded a Beit scholarship, but was unable to accept it as his father moved to Brandfort in the Orange Free State. Verwoerd senior took up the position of second minister and augmented his income by running a small bookshop. In February 1919[12] Hendrik Verwoerd matriculated and came first in the Orange Free State and fifth in South Africa.

---

10   J.J.J. Scholtz, *Die Moord Op Dr. Verwoerd*, Nasionale Boekhandel Bpk, Kaapstad, 1967, 73. Verwoerd's favourite book was a fantasy story, *Puck of Pook's Hill*, written by Rudyard Kipling in 1906. When he wrote his book in 1967, Scholtz was assistant editor and political reporter of *Die Burger*. He later became foreign editor after spending a year on a Nieman Fellowship at Harvard University. Liberal Afrikaners were sent by the United States South Africa Leader Exchange Program (USSALEP) – a Rothschild/Rockefeller front – to America. The purpose of these programmes was to brainwash these Afrikaners into persuading their people to accept the inevitability of Black rule.
11   *Ibid.*, 73.
12   The matriculation examinations were delayed on account of the Spanish influenza epidemic.

Chapter II

ACADEMIA

In March 1919 Hendrik Verwoerd enrolled at the University of Stellenbosch which at that time was the scholastic centre of Afrikaner nationalism.[13] He took up residence at Dagbreek hostel and studied for a B.A. degree with the intention of becoming a *dominee* (clergyman). He was a brilliant student, frequently obtaining 100% in his exams, and possessed an incredible photographic memory. He graduated in 1921 with honours.

The Ouhoofgebou (Old Main Building) where Dr. Verwoerd studied and taught as Professor of Sociology. The building was completed in 1886 and was designed in the Cape Classical style by Carl Otto Hager. This photograph was taken in 1958.

The following year he changed direction and studied psychology under Professor R.W. Wilcocks for an M.A. with sociology and logic as complementary subjects. The title of his thesis was *Denkprosesse en die*

---
13   G. Allighan, *op.cit.*, xvi.

Dr. and Mrs. Verwoerd with their first motor car, a 1930 six-cylinder Studebaker Erskine.

Probleem van Waardes (Thought Processes and the Problem of Values). He was awarded his degree *cum laude* in 1923. In that same year he was elected chairman of the Students Representative Council. He was also chairman of the Debating Union and Philosophical Society and an active member of the Drama Society. For recreation he enjoyed hiking and playing tennis. He was awarded a Sir Abe Bailey bursary of £400 per year for three years at the University of Oxford, but declined it as he preferred to study psychology in Europe.

In 1924 Hendrik Verwoerd continued with his studies at Stellenbosch and at the end of that year was awarded a D.Phil degree *cum laude*. The title of his thesis was *Eksperimentele Studie van die Afstomping van Gemoedsdoeninge* (Experimental Study of the Blunting of the Emotions). It was the first doctorate to be written in Afrikaans at the university. At the same time he was appointed a temporary lecturer in logic.

In 1926 with the assistance of a smaller Croll and Gray bursary of £150, Dr. Verwoerd travelled to Europe in order to pursue his studies at the universities of Berlin, Hamburg and Leipzig. At the last named university he spent a semester studying ethnic psychology at the Leipzig Institute of Experimental Psychology under Professors Otto Klem, Felix Krüger and Hans Volket.[14] While he was in Germany Dr. Verwoerd married Betsie Schoombie in Hamburg on 7 January 1927. They would subsequently have seven children. Thereafter Dr. Verwoerd continued his studies in Britain and the United States.

On his return to South Africa in 1927 Dr. Verwoerd was appointed Professor

---
14 C. Marx, Hendrik Verwoerd and the Leipzig School of Psychology, *Historia,* 58, 2, November 2013, 91-118. http://www.scielo.org.za/pdf/hist/v58n2/05.pdf

of Applied Psychology, Sociology and Social Science at the University of Stellenbosch. He would occupy this post for the next nine years. Dr. Verwoerd gave his lectures in the Ou Hoofgebou.[15] Although he prepared his lectures in the evening, he never used notes; but nonetheless gave stimulating lessons and was very popular with his students.[16] In 1929 he gave the opening speech at the commencement of the academic year and in 1932 was appointed head of the department of sociology and social work.

Professor Hendrik Verwoerd at the University of Stellenbosch, circa 1933.

During this period Dr. Verwoerd concerned himself with the 'poor white' problem. At a national congress held in Kimberley in 1934 he campaigned for the establishment of a government department of social welfare and was appointed chairman of the continuation committee. He served for two years

---
15 In 1967-1969 the author attended lectures in English, Latin and Roman-Dutch Law in the Ou Hoofgebou.
16 J. J. Scholtz, *op.cit.*, 75.

on the Organisation for Housing in Cape Town and became a co-director of the Good Hope Model Housing Scheme. He also testified as an expert witness before the Commission on the Coloureds.

On 27 October 1936 a meeting, billed as *The Jewish Danger*, was held in the Recreation Hall at Stellenbosch University. It was attended by 1,500 people and addressed by Professors Christian Schumann and Johannes Basson and Dr. Eben Dönges. A few days later when the Nord-Deutscher Lloyd steamship, *Stuttgart*, which had been chartered by the London based Council for German Jewry, docked in Cape Town harbour with 545 refugees on board, Dr. Verwoerd and the three aforementioned academics held up placards protesting their arrival. [17] Dr. Verwoerd was against Jewish immigration, as he believed that these Jews would aggravate the poor White problem and hamper the economic development of the Afrikaner.

In 1937 Prime Minister JBM Hertzog introduced the Aliens Bill in order to curtail immigration of Jews, while Dr. D F Malan, the leader of the *Gesuiwerde Nasionale Party* (Purified National Party), tabled an amendment prohibiting the entry of all Jewish immigrants, who were allegedly fleeing Germany because of "persecution".[18] Their immigration was to a certain extent also resented by the local Jewish community, who were aware that too many Jews would upset the racial balance between Whites and Jews. At that time there were 90,645 Jews in South Africa comprising 4.5% of the White population.[19]

---

17 J. Botha, *Verwoerd is Dead*, Books of Africa (Pty.) Ltd, Cape Town, 1967, 10. See also *Verwoerd só onthou ons hom*, compiled by Wilhelm J. Verwoerd, Protea Boekhuis, Pretoria, 2001, 13, 44 and M. Shain, *A Perfect Storm: Antisemitism in South Africa 1930-1948*, Jonathan Ball Publishers, Cape Town, 2015, 132-134.
18 It needs to be noted that it was the Jews who first created problems for themselves by adopting an openly antagonistic attitude towards the National Socialists. Within seven weeks of assuming power, the following provocative headline appeared in the 24 March 1933 edition of the London *Daily Express*, JUDEA DECLARES WAR ON GERMANY Boycott of German Goods.
19 http://www.jewishsa.co.za/about-sajbd/sa-jewish-history/

Chapter III

Editor Of Die Transvaler

In 1936 the directors of the Voortrekkerpers under the chairmanship of Mr. W.A. Hofmeyr, invited Dr. Verwoerd to become editor of a new Afrikaans daily newspaper, *Die Transvaler*. Prior to his departure for Johannesburg, Dr. Verwoerd spent a few months at the offices of the Cape Town newspaper, *Die Burger*, familiarising himself with journalism and office management. His task was not only to establish a newspaper, but to help rebuild the National Party.

His editorship also provided him with an opportunity to make his views more widely known among the public and to thereby enhance his prospects of fulfilling a more prominent role in the National Party. In 1938 he was elected deputy chairman of the board of control and management committee of the National Party. One of the first leading editorial articles in *Die Transvaler* was titled *Die Joodse Vraagstuk van die Nasionalistiese Standpunt* (The Jewish Question from the Nationalist Point of View).

In 1937 Anton Rupert, who later became a tobacco merchant, applied for a position as a reporter. He was offered a job, but later rejected it, as he said that he would have to study [20] by correspondence. Rupert would later become an arch enemy of Dr. Verwoerd and played a leading role in the plan to assassinate him.[21]

The majority of Afrikaners, as well as a fair number of English-speaking South Africans were against South Africa's participation in World War II, whose sole purpose was to destroy the usury-free banking systems of Germany, Italy and Japan. Dr. Verwoerd identified himself with this anti-war sentiment and was very outspoken in his condemnation of General Smuts, who was a pawn of the Zionists[22] and the international bankers.[23]

---

20 Rupert studied chemistry at the University of Pretoria.
21 P.J. Pretorius, Volksverraad, Libanon-Uitgewers, Mosselbaai, 1996, 156-165. In E. Dommisse, *Anton Rupert*, Tafelberg Publishers, Cape Town, 2005, 168, Rupert recalled that "as editor of *Die Transvaler*, Verwoerd had uttered not a word when the Nazis bombed Rotterdam and occupied the Netherlands in the Second World War, imposing dreadful hardship on that small country and killing many Dutch people. Verwoerd expressed no sign of public sympathy for the land of his birth in its hour of need". The bombing of Rotterdam, which was a fortified city, was an unfortunate accident. On account of the extraordinary delay which the Dutch took in agreeing to a surrender, a bombing attack, which had already been sanctioned, could not be recalled as long range radio communication was not in use at that time. The Germans placed red flares which sent back the first two waves of 24 bombers, but then ran out of these flares. In desperation the Germans used white flares, but this did not prevent the third wave of 12 bombers from coming through. See S. Goodson, Moral Equivalence & the Bombings of Rotterdam & Dresden, *The Barnes Review*, Vol. X No. 5, Washington D.C., September/October 2004, 52-53.
22 S.M. Goodson, *General Jan Christian Smuts The Debunking of a Myth*, Bienedell Publishers, Pretoria, 2013, 33-35.
23 S.M. Goodson, op.cit., 31. In October 1941 Smuts "donated" 54 tons of South Africa's gold reserves valued at £20 million (£128 billion in to-day's values) at Churchill's request in order to shore up Britain's crumbling finances. Smuts consulted neither his cabinet colleagues nor parliament. One month later the *USS Quincy*, a cruiser with a top speed of 33 knots, collected the gold at Simon's Town and shipped it via Trinidad to New York, where it was deposited into Rothschild's privately-owned US Federal Reserve Bank. During 1941 there was a temporary peak in gold production of 450 tons and thus the request for 54 tons was easily accommodated out of current production. See C.J.H. Hartnady, South Africa's gold production and reserves, *South African Journal of Science* 105, September/October 2009, 328.

Dr. Verwoerd in his office at *Die Transvaler*
which he edited from 1937 to 1948.

Dr. Verwoerd along with Dr. Malan did not accept the *bona fides* of a resistance movement called the *Ossewa Brandwag* (Ox wagon Sentinel), which had been set up as a cultural organisation in November 1938. He objected to their pointless acts of sabotage and frequently attacked its leaders in his columns. There is a strong possibility that Dr. Verwoerd may have suspected that the *Ossewa Brandwag* was a false front, which indeed it was. It had been set up by Smuts's former Secretary of Justice, Johannes Fredrik Janse van Rensburg in order to lure discontented Afrikaners into a fake cause which Smuts could monitor and control.[24] One of the *agents provocateurs* employed by Smuts was B.J. Vorster,[25] who would later take on a pivotal role in Dr Verwoerd's assassination, and in the dismantling of his policy of separate development.

On 22 October 1941 at midnight an attempt was made by two masked *stormjaers* (assailants of the *Ossewa Brandwag*), armed with a pistol and a sawn-off shotgun, to kidnap Dr. Verwoerd. They had orders to have him court-martialled and then taken into the veld where he would have been sjambokked (whipped). Fortunately a *stormjaer* in custody had tipped off the police and a car full of Special Branch police arrived just in time to prevent the kidnapping taking place.[26]

---

24   P.J. Pretorius, *op.cit.*, 102-108.
25   *Ibid.*, 142-147.
26   Allighan, *op. cit., xxiii*.

In the general election of 17 July 1943 Dr. Verwoerd was offered an opportunity to stand in a safe seat, but the leader of the National Party in the Transvaal, Advocate Johannes Gerhardus Strydom, asked him to stay on as editor of *Die Transvaler* where he would be more effective in promoting the cause of the party.

On 31 January 1947 at the invitation of General Smuts, the British Royal Family arrived in Cape Town aboard the battleship *HMS Vanguard* for a three month tour of South Africa and its surrounding territories. Dr. Verwoerd considered the tour to be a ploy by Smuts, which the latter hoped would improve his prospects of being re-elected in the following year's general election. The visit would moreover retard the National Party's aim of achieving a republic. As Dr. Verwoerd could do nothing about the Royal tour, he decided to ignore it, even though the leader of the National Party in Transvaal, Advocate J.G. Strijdom was against such a decision. The only report which appeared in *Die Transvaler* was a solitary paragraph: "The presence of certain visitors today will cause some dislocation of the traffic".[27] This was a repetition of a previous incident of antipathy towards the Royal family which took place in Stellenbosch in May 1925, when Dr. Verwoerd, who was at that time a lecturer in psychology, refused to attend a reception held in honour of the Prince of Wales.[28]

---

[27] *Ibid.*, xxi. Instead the leading article was written about the drought. 52 of Dr. Verwoerd's leading articles may be found in O. Geyser (Compiler), *Dr. H.F. Verwoerd die Republikein, Hoofartikels uit Die Transvaler 1937-1948*, Institut vir Eietydse Geskiedenis, U.O.V.S., Tafelberg-Uitgewers, Kaapstad, 1972, 100 pp.

[28] Verwoerd *só onthou ons hom, op.cit.*, 41-42. At the reception the Prince received a sympathetic tribute from a young Afrikaner who stood up and said, "We cheered because we know a man when we see one. Our presence here is intended as a tribute to your manliness which the most persistent attempts of the whole world have not been able to spoil". H. Bolitho, *King Edward VIII – Duke of Windsor*, Peter Owen Limited, London, 1954, 127.

Chapter IV

MINISTER OF NATIVE AFFAIRS (1950-1958)

In the general election held on 26 May 1948 Dr. Verwoerd stood in the Transvaal constituency of Alberton, but lost narrowly by 171 votes. Nonetheless the National Party won the election by 79 to 71 seats. Dr. Verwoerd was elected to the Senate as a representative of Transvaal and soon became party whip. In 1950 he became leader of the Nationalists in the Senate. In October of that year he was appointed Minister of Native Affairs, replacing Dr. E.G. Jansen who was elevated to the position of Governor-General. Once he had accepted the post, Dr. Verwoerd undertook a deep study of Bantu institutions, traditions and thought processes. His expertise in psychology and the use of vivid imagery enable him to communicate with African people with great facilitation.[29] Later he would encourage his officials to learn at least one African language. During the 1930s Dr. Verwoerd had a played a key role in the resolution of the poor white problem. Dr. Verwoerd believed that this experience would stand him in good stead in his ambitious desire to uplift all the Bantu people of South Africa.[30]

300 YEAR HISTORY OF APARTHEID[31]

It has been claimed that Dr. Verwoerd was the architect of apartheid, but this is incorrect. Eighty percent of the so called apartheid laws[32] were promulgated by the Dutch and British colonial governments between 1652 and 1910. For example in 1685 Governor Simon van der Stel passed a law prohibiting miscegenation between the different races, while on 4 November 1808 the Earl of Caledon introduced the first pass laws, the *Hottentot Code*. [33]This ordinance was later succeeded by the Kaffir Pass Act and Kaffir Employment Act of 1857. On 17 December 1847 Sir Harry Smith, Governor of the Cape Colony, established the first Bantustan, British Kaffraria. In terms of Section XIX (4) of the London Convention of 27 February 1884, signed by the High Commissioner for Southern Africa, Sir Hercules Robinson, natives were "allowed to move freely within the country [South African Republic], or to leave it for any legal purpose, under a pass system". In 1905 Sir Godfrey Yeatman Lagden, chairman of the South African Native Affairs Commission, drew up a report which recommended the separation of Black South Africans and White South Africans as occupiers of land and as voters. The report was adopted by Lord Alfred Milner, the Governor of the Transvaal and Orange River Colony.

---

29   F. Barnard. *op.cit.*, 46.
30   J.J. Scholtz, *op.cit.*, 78.
31   The correct translation in English is separateness.
32   J. A. Marais, *op. cit.*, 32. See also R. Lacour-Gayet, *The History of South Africa*, Cassell & Co. Ltd, London, 1977, 384 pp. According to this French professor of history, apartheid was introduced as a government policy in 1834.
33   M. van Bart, *Kaap Van Slawe*, Historical Media cc, Tokai, South Africa, 2012, 114.

Du Pre Alexander, 2nd Earl of Caledon was governor of the Cape of Good Hope (1806-1811). On 4 November 1808 he introduced the first pass laws by government proclamation.

A further 10% of the apartheid, or more correctly separate development laws, such as the Natives Land Act of 1913[34] and the Natives Trust and Land Act of 1936 were passed by the Botha-Smuts-Hertzog administrations. The latter act granted 13% of the country's land, which included the richest platinum mines in the world, to the indigenous population. The number of hectares allocated in the new law increased by 150% from six million to 15 million. It also needs to be pointed out that these territories consisted of some of the most fertile regions with a high rainfall and may be juxtaposed to the fact that over 30% of white land was semi-desert.

One further factor which provides a more accurate perspective, is that if one includes the three former High Commission protectorates of Basutoland, Bechuanaland and Swaziland, which form an integral part of Southern Africa south of the Limpopo River, the land owned by African people of this region rises to 50%.[35] In a speech he gave on 3 September 1963, when opening the Transvaal Congress of the National Party in Pretoria, Dr. Verwoerd suggested,

---

34 Although the Act designated only 7% of the land to Blacks, that was the land that they were occupying at that time, it contained two important exemptions. Land already owned by Blacks in White areas could be retained and land also could be acquired in these White areas by means of an exemption. Between 1924 and 1936, 565 exemptions were granted. http://www.bdlive.co.za/articles/2010/03/11/jacob-dlamini-was-natives-land-act-sa-s-original-political-sin

35 *Verwoerd aan die Woord,* edited by Prof. A.N. Pelser, Afrikaanse-Pers Boekhandel, Johannesburg, 1966, 268.

in an act of good neighbourliness, that the Protectorates should be allowed to develop to independence under South Africa's guardianship and added that: "I am sure that if we put our case to them they would wish us to be their guardians". He believed that South Africa "could lead them far better and quicker to independence and economic prosperity than Britain can".[36] He reiterated that South Africa had no territorial ambitions over the Protectorates, but that it had a very indirect interest in that it wanted good and prosperous neighbours. This was in line with Dr. Verwoerd's policy that South Africa did not wish to be the leader of Africa, but wished rather to co-operate with other nations and be a provider of knowledge, service and aid.[37]

Whereas in North America[38] and Australasia the indigenous populations were largely eradicated, this was not the case in Southern Africa. The Whites protected the Blacks and if that protection had not been given, they may well have been very few Black people living in the region today.[39] Furthermore the Whites also prevented the Black tribes from exterminating each other.[40]

The first two prime ministers of South Africa Generals Louis Botha and Jan Smuts were firm supporters of separate development as the following quotations reveal.

Louis Botha said the following:

"The placing of the races on an equal footing will never bring about satisfaction and therefore another direction must be taken…that the solution is to be found in the expansion of the rights of the natives. One must give these people a certain amount of self-government – under the supervision of the whites naturally…so that they can work themselves upwards".[41]

"The kaffir[42] question was the most difficult of all, but he believed that it could be solved by separating the kaffirs into certain areas and giving them the right to self-determination – but nowhere else".[43]

"The whites must adopt a very careful attitude in connection with the natives…they bear the responsibility to develop these people. Separation is only to the advantage of the native…If the natives are separated, they must

---

36 S.E.D. Brown, *Verwoerd's Dramatic Appeal On Protectorates*, *The South African Observer,* September 1963, 16.
37 *Verwoerd aan die Woord, op.cit.*, 568-569.
38 In 1620 there were 6 million Red Indians in North America, to-day there are only 3 million plus 2 million half breeds; in South Africa, where there were an estimated one million Blacks in 1652, to-day there are over 44 million.
39 *Verwoerd aan die Woord, op.cit.,* 354.
40 *Ibid.,* 602.
41 *Ibid.,* xxx.
42 *Ibid.,* 278. Here Dr. Verwoerd confirms that he never used the pejorative term 'kaffir'.
43 *Ibid.,* xxx.

be given the right to govern themselves. Let them govern themselves under the supervision of the white".[44]

The views of General Smuts were almost identical. In a speech titled *The White Man's Task*, which he delivered on 22 May 1917 while a member of the British Imperial War Cabinet, he said:

> "We have realised that political ideas which apply to our white civilisation largely do not apply to the administration of native affairs. To apply the same institutions on an equal basis to white and black alike does not lead to the best results, and so a practice has grown up in South Africa of creating parallel institutions – giving the natives their own separate institutions on parallel lines with institutions for whites. It may be that on those parallel lines we may yet be able to solve a problem which may otherwise be insoluble…We have felt more and more that if we are to solve our native question it is useless to try and govern black and white in the same system, to subject them to the same institutions of government and legislation. They are different not only in colour but in mind and in political capacity and their political institutions should be different, while always proceeding on the basis of self-government…We have now legislation before the Parliament of the Union in which an attempt is made… to create all over South Africa, wherever there are any considerable native communities, independent self-governing institutions for them. Thus in South Africa you will have in the long run large areas cultivated by blacks, where they will look after themselves in all their forms of living and development, while in the rest of the country you will have white communities, which will govern themselves separately according to accepted European principles."[45] In 1929 General Smuts repeated the same ideas and policies more emphatically at the Rhodes Memorial Lectures held at Oxford University.[46]

---

44 *Ibid.*, xxx.
45 *Ibid.*, xxx-xxxi.
46 *Ibid.*, xxxi.

Sir Theophilus Shepstone, Secretary for Native Affairs (1853-1875) in Natal, was highly respected by the Zulu people, who called him *Uysise* or Father. He strove for separation of the races and the maintenance of tribal custom.

It was not only leading Afrikaners who held such views. In Natal, Sir Theophilus Shepstone the Secretary for Native Affairs (1853-1875), who spoke fluent Xhosa and Zulu, first introduced the policy of apartheid which he called separation.[47] The main focus of his policy was on maintaining tribal customs and not to enforce white civilisation. In a parliamentary debate on the Natives Land Act in April 1913, a member of the Unionist Party, Sir Patrick Duncan, who was later appointed Governor-General in 1937, said that "everyone would agree with the principle enunciated by the Minister that it was to the best interests of Europeans and natives that points of social contact should be reduced to the least possible area".[48] Separate racial development had been standard practice since the inception of Britain's colonial era.[49] The Lord Lugard, Governor-General of Nigeria (1913-1918) first introduced separate development in British colonial West Africa. "Lugard's policy was that the African peoples' own social and political institutions, the product of centuries of accumulated experience and wisdom, should be preserved, strengthened and modernised in an evolutionary manner".[50] One of Lord Lugard's favourite dicta was, "Never try to turn the African Black into an Oxford Blue!"[51]

---

47   http://www.britannica.com/biography/Theophilus-Shepstone
48   Debates, House of Assembly, 1913, Col. 2287.
49   A.T. Culwick, South Africa Is A Great Country, Says Kenya Immigrant, *The South African Observer*, October 1962, 9.
50   This line of thinking has been supported and actively encouraged by the famous Zulu sangoma, Credo Mutwa. See also S.M. Goodson, *Rhodesian Prime Minister Ian Smith The Debunking of a Myth*, Self-published, Cape Town, 2015, 51.
51   A.T. Culwick, *op.cit.*, 9.

Sir Patrick Duncan (1870-1943), a cabinet minister and later Governor-General of the Union of South Africa, enunciated in parliament in 1913 the principle "that it was to the best interests of Europeans and natives that points of social contact should be reduced to the least possible area".

SEPARATE DEVELOPMENT

Thus we may perceive that the structure of parallel or separate development had already been firmly laid down by Dr. Verwoerd's predecessors over the previous 300 years. Dr. Verwoerd was only responsible for refining the parameters and shaping them into a coherent and workable policy. The National Party codified many of the existing customary conventions and practices such as the Immorality Act of 1949,[52] Prohibition of Mixed Marriages Act of 1949 and the Group Areas Act of 1950 which provided for separate residential areas. Dr. Verwoerd also replaced passes with identity books. The purpose of these identity books was to protect existing workers from the influx of non-urban blacks and illegal immigrants, who would force wages down and reduce their living standards.[53] All these laws were designed to protect the indigenous population rather than to harm them.

In a speech[54] he gave to the South Africa Club on 17 March 1961, Dr. Verwoerd explained that when the first settlers arrived they did not come as colonists or colonisers and that they only occupied vacant land. They first encountered black people at the Great Fish River in the Eastern Cape in 1779 and did not

---

52 This was an amendment to the original Immorality Act of 1927. The Orange Free State and British colonies introduced a number of similar laws in the pre-Union period.
53 J.A. Marais, *op.cit.*, 22.
54 *Verwoerd aan die Woord, op.cit.*, 474.

appropriate any of their areas. Contrary to what happened to the indigenous people in the Americas, they were not eradicated. Blacks did not develop themselves and therefore sought along with black foreigners work in white areas, food and the benefits of civilisation, such as health services and security and did not demand any political rights. Moreover, they were often fleeing from tyranny and internecine tribal warfare. The immigration of black workers into urban areas had to a great extent been spurred on by the expansion of the mining sector and industrialisation which had taken place during the world wars.

In his maiden speech[55] as a senator on 3 September 1948, Dr. Verwoerd laid down the broad parameters of the policy of Separate Development. He described it as a middle path between total integration[56] and total segregation, in the realisation that territorial segregation was not possible.[57] Whites and blacks would only be able to own land in their respective territories. In the cities there would be separate residential areas for each racial group and each group would be allowed to have local government structures. In the factories white and non-white would work apart where possible and certain occupations would be reserved for whites. Replacing poverty in the homelands with misery in the cities was not a solution; therefore influx control would be strengthened and as the economies of the native reserves developed, the flow of migrants would slowly reverse itself. Dr. Verwoerd pointed out that migrant labour in the urban and mining areas was similar to the 3,000,000 seasonal labourers from Italy who worked in France, but did not enjoy any political rights. Another analogy he employed was by turning the Eurasian landmass 90 degrees to the left and then comparing the whites in the southern most portion of Africa to the Europeans who inhabited the southern portion of this landmass.[58]

He often referred to the example of Basutoland (Lesotho) whose population had remained static since 1910, because its inhabitants were constantly migrating to South Africa in search of work. Basutoland's function as a provider of migratory labour was little different from how South Africa's Bantustans also provided labour.[59]

---

55 *Ibid.*, 1-16.
56 In Dr. Verwoerd's opinion integration is a form of genocide to both Black and White.
57 It should be noted that Dr Verwoerd was prepared to compromise on this principle and accept a smaller White state with its own army, navy and police force. See J.A. Marais, op.cit., 57 and *Verwoerd aan die Woord, op.cit.*, 265.
58 *Verwoerd aan die Woord, op.cit.*, 469.
59 *Ibid.*, 110.

Dr. Verwoerd's first legislative acts were concessions which were designed to ameliorate the position of the Bantu. The Native Abolition of Passes and Co-ordination of Documents Act of 1952 abolished all regional passes and introduced a standard identity document, while the Native Laws Amendment Act of the same year allowed a Black person, who had been in the service of one employer for ten years or had had lawful employment in the area for 15 years to remain in an urban area for 72 hours without a permit.

TOMLINSON COMMISSION

In 1950 F.R. Tomlinson, professor of agricultural economics at the University of Stellenbosch, was appointed to make a thorough survey of the socio-economic development of the native reserves. Although the work of the *Commission for the Socio-Economic Development of the Bantu Areas within the Union of South Africa* was completed in 1954, it was only on 14 May 1956 that Dr. Verwoerd discussed the report in parliament.[60]

The Commission proposed the establishment of a number of Bantu homelands. In order to absorb the population increase in the reserves, it was recommended that improved agricultural practices be adopted and that the population be spread more evenly over the designated territories. It also recommended that the homelands should be industrialised with white capital, as part of an overall national policy of decentralisation.[61] This was one of the two points on which Dr. Verwoerd differed; the other being the replacement of communal tenure of agricultural land with individual tenure, which would undermine the authority of the chiefs. He said that it was not only immoral to employ white capital, but that it would necessitate providing security of tenure to the white owners and result in whites having to settle in the proximity of the industrial areas in the homelands.[62]

The matter was resolved by the setting up industries[63] which were located up to 30 miles (50km) distant from the borders of the homelands. These border industries were financed with white capital and were granted financial incentives such as subsidised railway rates and tax concessions. These industries were generally labour intensive. Bantu workers were able to commute daily to their place of work and live with their families which was an important factor in promoting social stability. They were also able to spend a portion of their income in the homelands.[64]

---

60   J. Botha, *op.cit.*, 23. It contained 3,755 pages, 598 tables and 66 maps.
61   *Verwoerd aan die Woord, op.cit.*, 95-114.
62   *Ibid.*, xlv-xlvii.
63   *Ibid.*, 629.
64   *Ibid.*, 599-609.

In the 1951 census the breakdown of the different racial groups was given as follows:

	Million	%
Bantu	8.5	67.5
European	2.6	20.6
Coloured	1.2	9.5
Indian	.3	2.4
TOTAL	12.6	100.0

BANTU TOWNSHIPS

During World War II when many new industries, particularly on the Witwatersrand, were established, the United Party government had allowed hundreds of thousands of blacks to stream into the urban areas without providing them with proper accommodation and amenities. Dr. Verwoerd's Department of Native Affairs embarked on a massive programme of slum clearance, replacing these hideous eyesores with neatly laid out townships with houses built on a plot and service scheme basis. Each plot had a garden and each township had a dedicated railway connection.[65] The townships were divided into ethnic areas so as to prevent friction and to facilitate the provision of mother tongue education. Liaison officers were appointed to maintain links with the respective homelands.

The financing of these townships was undertaken by government and was supplemented by levies[66] (2s. 6d. per week) paid by employers on behalf of their black employees in terms of the Bantu Services Levy Act of 1952. As the whites paid 90% of the taxes at that time, they were the ultimate source of these funds. This was adumbrated by General Hertzog during the debate on the Native Trust and Land Act of 1936, when he said that if the whites desire segregation, they will have to pay for it.[67] Dr. Verwoerd frequently stressed that the non-white population is an important and valuable economic factor and that their place in the country's economy and the acquisition of the greatest possible welfare had to be recognised. In their own interest and in order to maintain the most harmonious co-operation with the whites, it would have to take place with recognition of the vital social boundaries.

---

65 *Ibid.*, 89.
66 Bantu Services Levy Act of 1952.
67 *Verwoerd aan die Woord, op.cit.*, xxxii.

Bantu Homelands

Regarding the native reserves, Dr. Verwoerd said that additional land would only be granted under the Act of 1936 after a judicious and thorough investigation.[68] More land was not the solution as it would be overgrazed.[69] What was needed was a change in methods of agriculture. A vigorous campaign against overgrazing and soil erosion would be undertaken. The reserves would be provided with schools and improved social, health and welfare services. The blacks would provide their own police, post office and railway officials, school teachers and social workers.[70] The Bantu Authorities Act of 1951 created the legal basis for self-determination of the various ethnic and linguistic tribes and traditional homeland reserves and established tribal, regional and territorial authorities. Seven radio stations were established for the different African languages. This ability to govern themselves would engender pride in their achievements and their homeland. Dr. Verwoerd believed that the homelands could support a much higher population. In a speech in parliament on 14 May 1956 he said that Pondoland in the Eastern Cape, which has an area of 120,421 square miles (311,888 square kilometres) could sustain a population of 19 million, if it were governed by Europeans, such as Belgians, Danes or Italians.[71] In order to stimulate industrialisation, the Bantu Investment Corporation was established on 3 June 1959 with a capital of R2 million. It financed commercial and industrial enterprises in the homelands and by 1963 had granted 339 loans with a value of R1.07 million.

Group Areas Act

In 1950 the Group Areas Act was promulgated and was followed by the Separate Amenities Act in 1953. The Group Areas Act was a source of contention, particularly amongst the Coloured and Indian communities. The removal of the inhabitants of District Six on the outskirts of the centre of the city of Cape Town from 1966 onwards caused much protest, but it was justified, as the area had become an overcrowded, unsanitary and unsafe slum, which had been condemned by health authorities for decades. Furthermore over half of the properties were owned by Jewish slumlords.

Under British colonial rule in the Cape a regulation was introduced that decreed on each title deed that a Coloured person was not permitted to live on White owned land, while in 1902 the Native Reserve Location Act segregated Africans into separate residential areas.

---

[68] *Ibid.*, 28. 7,250,000 morgen (4,478,785 acres) was granted in terms of the 1936 Act, but this land soon became overpopulated and was not used productively.
[69] 90% of prime farming land handed over to Blacks since 1994 has been destroyed. http://www.voanews.com/content/black-farmers-in-south-africa-still-struggling-with-land-reform/1535152.html. See also P. du Toit, *The Great South African Land Scandal*, Legacy Publications, Centurion, Pretoria, 2004, 200 pp.
[70] *Verwoerd aan die Woord, op.cit.*, 140.
[71] *Ibid.*, 110.

The Group Areas Act was not enforced dogmatically. A mile to the west of District Six the Malay Quarter of Bo-Kaap/Schotsche Kloof, nestled below Signal Hill, was left undisturbed. It has been occupied by Cape Malays since 1790 when the Dutch East India Company granted them permission to reside there. The Act also stipulated they no one could be removed until alternative accommodation had been provided and compensation had to be paid for all properties acquired. An amount of R30 million was spent in respect of the relocation of the 60,000 Coloureds of District Six, who were principally of Malay ethnicity and Moslem by religion.

Coloured Affairs

In a speech given[72] on 12 December 1961 to the Council for Coloured Affairs, which was in effect the Coloured parliament, Dr. Verwoerd explained his four stream policy which was applicable to each race, as well as the finer points of the Group Areas Act. He provided Europe as an example, where there are only small racial differences and even though they have the same morphology, origins, knowledge and customs, they prefer to live apart[73] and retain their own heritage. He said that borders bring fewer conflicts and that human dignity is promoted by co-existence and not by living together.[74] Dr. Verwoerd undertook not only to promote the economic welfare of the Coloured people, but he promised to protect them. He warned them that they would be the first to be adversely affected in a multi-racial government.[75] His speech was received with much enthusiasm by the Coloured leaders and in his word of thanks, the Chairman expressed high praise for what Dr. Verwoerd was doing and planning to do for the Coloured people. Dr. Verwoerd received a standing ovation.[76] By means of the Coloured Persons Representative Council Act of 1964, provision was made for the election of 40 members and 20 nominated members. Five members served on the executive.

Indian Affairs

Repatriation of the Indian community had been a policy objective of the National Party since 1948. In 1961 Dr. Verwoerd announced that this policy had been abandoned and that Indians were deemed to be a permanent part of South Africa's population. In 1966 a National Indian Council was established as a non-statutory body with 20 appointed members. In 1968 it was given statutory standing and was renamed the South African Indian Council and consisted of 25 members.

---

72 *Ibid.*, 599-609.
73 For example, with exception of Brussels, Belgium has a *taalgrens* or language border which separates the two main population groups, the Flemings and the Walloons.
74 J.A. Marais, *op.cit.*, 64-65.
75 *Verwoerd aan die Woord, op.cit.*, 602-603.
76 *Ibid.*, 599.

Bantu Education

In 1950 when Dr. Verwoerd assumed the Native Affairs portfolio, he also asked that Bantu education be transferred from the department of education to his department, as it complemented his portfolio. He was fully aware of the racial-biological differences between the races[77] and that one cannot change the inherent nature of Blacks and their inability to plan for the long term, which is reflected in their languages having only a present tense, no past or future tenses and a very limited vocabulary. Separate systems of education were thus indispensable for the advancement of each racial group, and in particular for the Bantu people. These differences may not only be observed in skin colour and morphology, but primarily in their biological make-up. Thus it has been proven scientifically that the average weight of a White brain is 1,413 gm,[78] while that of a Black is 1,249 gm.[79] The average cubic capacity of a White brain is 1,481 cu. cm. and that of a Black is 1,316 cu.cm. The cerebral cortex is thicker, the gyri more complicated and the sulci are deeper in the case of white brains.[80] The cortex governs the most advanced types of mental activity such as mathematical ability and other forms of abstract reasoning. The frontal lobe[81] of the White forebrain is more developed than that of a Black person. Thus the latter's ability in the performance of thinking, planning, communication and behaviour is more limited than that of Whites. Even more important than brain size are differences in brain shape, fissuration, the number of pyramidal neurons and super-granular layer thickness. It has been proven that the depth of fissuration is related to superior intelligence and that the brains of Whites have deeper fissures in the frontal and occipital regions. The discovery in April 2012 by an international team of scientists of the gene HMGA2, which determines brain size and intelligence, has confirmed the supremacy of the racial-determinant view of intelligence and achievement and completely displaces the nurture and culture argument of the followers of the Jewish pseudo-scientist Franz Uri Boas.

---

77 *Ibid.*, xxxv and 61. In a speech given in the Senate on 7 June 1954, when he launched his Bantu Education policy, Dr. Verwoerd cited figures showing the inability of Black pupils to cope with the European education syllabus. Only 10% of the pupils passed Standard II, 3½% passed Standard VI, half a percent obtained the Junior Certificate and a very small number the Senior Certificate.

78 J. R. Baker, *Race*, Oxford University Press, 431.

79 C. Putnam, *Race and Reality,* Howard Allen Printing, Cape Canaveral, 1980, 84. This figure first appeared in an article written by Dr. J.H. Sequeira for *The British Medical Journal*, March 1932.

80 C.W.M. Poynter and J.J. Keegan, "A Study of the American Negro Brain", *Journal of Comparative Neurology*, Vol. 25, 1915, 183-212.

81 W.C. Halstead, Brains and Intelligence: A Qualitative Study of the Frontal Lobes, University of Chicago, 1947, 149. Halstead writes that "The frontal lobes are the portion of the brain most essential to biological intelligence. They are the organs of civilization - the basis of man's hope for the future".

These differences in brain structure are reflected in intelligence quotients which are the premier assessment of cognitive ability. Whites have an average of 100 and for Blacks the average is 70.[82] Although there is an overlap between the races, it is only 11% and would need to be 50% for there to be equality. For both the maintenance and advancement of any civilisation, IQs of 160+ are absolutely vital if there is to be a sufficient number of engineers, inventors, mathematicians, scientists etc., and these high IQs are only to be found in the White race. Heritability is the dominant factor, with environment playing only a minor role.[83] Professor Arthur Robert Jensen of the Psychology Department of the University of Berkeley California showed in his monumental work *Bias in Mental Testing* (786 pages) that the questions in IQ tests provide equally reliable readings of Blacks' and Whites' abilities. Poverty is not an adequate explanation for the Black-White IQ gap, because it is as wide as it is among the indigent of all races.

Prior to 1954, when the Bantu Education Act was promulgated, black education was mostly in the hands of the churches and missionary societies. Although these bodies received a 100% state subsidy, the progress they had evinced in the education of black children had been poor. The primary focus of these schools had been to turn as many blacks as possible into educated Europeans, who would have aspirations in a society where they had limited chances of success.[84] At the graduation ceremony of Fort Hare College in the Eastern Cape in May 1938, General Smuts expressed similar sentiments when he said: "The accepted policy of the country is not to impose European conditions and ways of thought and culture on Native peoples. There is something in the Native peoples worth developing. Native Africa has its contribution to bring to the world and we should be doing a disservice forcing on them the European's own exotic views and culture".[85] Dr. Verwoerd wished to expand the education system so that everyone could benefit and not select individuals. The previous education system kept the majority of black school children in a primitive state[86] with diminished expectations of advancement and did not prepare them for service in their communities effectively.[87] Furthermore this system was hindered by a lack of funds and the absence of a uniform, declared policy.

---

82 National IQ Scores compiled by Professors Richard Lynn, Tatu Vanhanen and Jelte Wicherts. http://www.photius.com/rankings/national_iq_scores_country_ranks.html

83 W. Flax, Environmentalism – Scientific 'Achilles Heel' of Collectivist Totalitarianism, *The Mankind Quarterly*, Edinburgh, Vol. VI, No. 4, Oct.-Dec. 1965 and R. Pearson, *Shockley on Eugenics and Race*, Scott-Townsend Publishers, Washington, D.C., 1992, 190-191 for an analysis of Professor Sir Cyril Burt's data on monozygotic white twins brought up in vastly different economic environments, but having identical IQs.

84 F. Barnard, *op.cit.*, 47.

85 P.B. Blanckenberg, *The Thoughts of General Smuts*, Juta & Co. Limited, Cape Town, 1951, 152.

86 *Verwoerd aan die Woord, op.cit.*, 82. According to the *Eybers Commission* on adult education of 1945, only 20% of the Bantu population was estimated to be literate at that time.

87 *Ibid.*, xliii.

The Bantu Education Act provided for a centralised and state controlled black educational system in unison with the Bantu people's traditions and customs.[88] For the first time black parents were given a say in their children's education by means of school boards and school committees. Strong emphasis was placed on mother tongue education,[89] and all teacher training colleges were placed under the department's control. Initially, on account of the shortage of schools, double sessions were introduced. Teachers repeated the same lessons in the mornings and afternoons to different sets of pupils. Free text books were provided, but had to be shared by two pupils until sufficient numbers of text books had been printed. In the high schools both the Joint Matriculation Board and Senior Certificate syllabi could be studied by Black pupils. The notion that Bantu education was inferior is thus false.[90]

The following year in 1955 left-wing agitators tried to organise a boycott on the Witwatersrand in which 7,000 school children stayed away. Dr. Verwoerd reacted quickly and told the parents that either the children returned to school immediately or he would close them permanently. Within ten days a delegation of parents came to ask him for forgiveness and said that they would not misbehave again by keeping their children at home, and would moreover take action against people or organisations who incited further action.[91]

By 1961 there were 4,000 parents serving on 496 school boards and more than 34,000 parents were serving on school committees. In 1963 there were 8,463 Bantu schools and 29,702 teachers at these schools. Between 1948 and 1963 expenditure on Bantu education increased by 194% from R8.5 million to R25 million.[92] In 1967 80% of Blacks in the age group seven to 20 were literate and 83% of those in the age group seven to 14 were attending school. As Black children became more literate, there was a tendency for some of them to look down on their illiterate parents. Dr. Verwoerd rectified that problem by introducing evening schools for adults.

Bantu education was a huge success and it gave Black people recognition for their educational achievements and genuine hope for the future.[93]

---

88   J.D.J. Hofmeyr and H. Hitzeroth, Differences in Facial Conformation of Four Sub-Groups of the Bantu of South Africa, *The Mankind Quarterly*, Edinburgh, Vol. II, No. 1, July-September 1961. In this study the authors highlight "the strong tendency to form tribes in the Bantu".
89   *Verwoerd aan die Woord, op.cit.*, 70.
90   *Verwoerd só onthou ons hom, op.cit.*, 175. The writer of this essay *Iets oor Bantu-Onderwys* (Something about Bantu-Education), Mr. G.J. Rousseau, was a fluent speaker of the North Sotho and Tswana languages and served as director-general of Bantu Education (1975-1982).
91   J. Botha, *op.cit.*, 23.
92   *Ibid.*, 139. This was a real increase as inflation during the period 1958-1963 averaged 1.78%. http://www.inflation.eu/inflation-rates/south-africa/historic-inflation/cpi-inflation-south-africa-1960.aspx.
93   See R. Dageda, Bantu education was better: academic, *The Sowetan*, 15 August 2013. Dr. Rabelani Dageda, a lecturer at the Wits Business School, writes that: "It was far better in terms of quality than the education our kids are receiving nowadays".

In 1959 the first non-White universities[94] under the new dispensation were established viz. the University of the North and the Medical University of Southern Africa. These institutions were followed by the University of the Western Cape (Coloured) in 1959, the University of Zululand in 1960, the University of Durban-Westville (Indian) in 1972, the University of Bophuthatswana in 1978, the Vista University in 1981 and the University of Venda in 1982. All these universities were equipped to the same high standards as those enjoyed by White universities.

---

94 The first Black university was established at Fort Hare, Alice, Eastern Cape in 1916.

Chapter V

PRIME MINISTER (1958-1966)

On 24 August 1958 Prime Minister Johannes Gerhardus Strijdom died in Cape Town after a long illness. As he was the leader of the National Party, a ballot was necessary in order to determine his successor. Initially Dr. Verwoerd did not make himself available as a candidate, and when he did, he refused to take part in the customary lobbying.[95] The other two candidates were the most senior cabinet minister, Advocate C. R. Swart,[96] Minister of Justice, and Dr. T.E. Dönges, Minister of the Interior. The caucus of the National Party, which consisted of the 176 members of parliament and senators, met on 2 September 1958. In the first round of voting, Dr. Verwoerd received 80 votes, Dr Dönges 52 votes and Advocate Swart 41 votes. In the second round Dr. Verwoerd received 98 votes against the 75 votes received by Dr. Dönges. In his acceptance speech Dr. Verwoerd remarked that he was just the uppermost point of a pyramid and that his ability to make headway was dependent on the strength of the base.[97]

The opposition United Party, which stood for a united South Africa under White rule or *baasskap* (domination), was generally hostile to Dr. Verwoerd's election. This negative attitude contrasted with the congratulations he received from Black leaders and people "from almost every corner of South Africa".[98] At a National Party meeting he said that "The Bantu were realising more and more that the old Voortrekker policy of granting their own areas to the different races was the right and best policy".[99]

The following evening in a speech broadcast to the nation, Dr. Verwoerd announced his great ideal of forging unity between the Afrikaans- and English-speaking peoples. He believed that the best method of attaining such an aim would be to have a republican form of government. Dr. Verwoerd realised that having a monarchical head of state was a divisive factor and that a republic would heal the wounds of the past.[100] Unity amongst the White population was vital if Black/White problems were to be resolved. Dr. Verwoerd pointed out that Great Britain did not have a constitution and that the British monarch, as head of state, had reserve powers which were also applicable to South Africa.[101]

---

95 Allighan, *op.cit.*, xxiii. Nonetheless Dr. Albert Hertzog did play an active role in gathering support for Dr. Verwoerd.
96 In 1965 the author met State President C.R. Swart at his residence *Westbrooke*, after having received an introduction from his private secretary, Mr. Andries L. Pretorius.
97 F. Barnard, *op.cit.*, 62.
98 J. Botha, *op.cit.*, 40.
99 *Ibid.*, 40.
100 *Verwoerd aan die Woord*, op.cit., 358.
101 *Ibid.*, 358.

On 27 January 1959 Dr Verwoerd announced a policy which would entail the gradual liberation of the Bantu homelands and their eventual attainment of full independence. The legislation was contained in the Promotion of Bantu Self-government Act of 1959. A Commissioner-General would be entrusted with the development of each assigned territory, of which there were potentially eight, into a self-governing state.

Establishment of a Republic

On 20 January 1960 Dr. Verwoerd announced in parliament that the government had decided to hold a referendum on whether South Africa should remain a self-governing British dominion, which owed allegiance to the British crown. In order to raise this significant event above party politics,[102] it had been decided that each White voter[103] would be given the opportunity to express him- or herself irrespective of party considerations. Even if only a small majority voted in favour of a republic, it would be acceptable. Dr. Verwoerd cited the narrow winning margin of 13 votes in parliament on 5 September 1939, when it was decided to declare war on Germany in World War II.[104]

He also revealed that the functions of the head of government (prime minister) and head of state would remain separate, so that the sovereignty of the people would be retained.[105] In the new republican form of government there would be give and take – the English-speakers would give up the monarchy, while the Afrikaans-speakers would not be given an executive president, as was the case in the Boer republics.[106] Furthermore the South African flag, coat of arms and national anthem would not be changed and South Africa would remain a member of the British Commonwealth.[107]

Dr. Verwoerd conducted an intensive campaign, speaking in Bloemfontein, Groblersdal, Lichtenburg, Port Elizabeth, Johannesburg, Pretoria, Windhoek and lastly at the Goodwood show grounds in Cape Town, speaking before crowds of 5,000, 10,000 and 15,000 people. In his final speech he advised his supporters that if they should win, they should celebrate their victory modestly, so as not to antagonise their opponents.

The referendum was held on 5 October 1960 and the question put to the voters was "Are you in favour of a Republic for the Union?" When Dr. Verwoerd

---

102 *Ibid.*, 306.
103 *Ibid.*, 307.
104 *Ibid.*, 445.
105 *Ibid.*, 310.
106 *Ibid.*, 378.
107 *Ibid.*, 409.

voted, he did not ask to be placed at the head of the queue, but stood in line like everyone else awaiting his turn to vote.

In a voter turnout of 90.7% of the registered voters, 850,458 (52.3%) voted "Yes" and 775,878 (47.7%) voted "No", giving the republicans a majority of 74,580 votes. On 7 October 1960 Dr. Verwoerd praised the voters for the maturity they had shown, but recognised that differences of opinion would remain. He said that "Deep down, however, there must be a common purpose and a national loyalty which keeps us one. It is my keen desire and firm object to try to lead our nation in such a way that,without sacrificing or compromising on principle, either the one party or the other, we need never again feel like two nations in one State".[108]

The Year 1960

1960 would be a watershed year for both Africa and South Africa. The European colonial powers were informed by the international bankers that the indigenous populations had reached such a state of development that it would only be fair to grant them their "independence" and *uhuru* (freedom), even though they had barely left the nursery stage of civilisation. This change in direction suited both parties. The colonial powers would save on the expense of having to subsidise and develop these colonies (which it was indeed their responsibility), while the international bankers led by the Rothschild syndicate would plunge these hapless territories into irredeemable and permanent debt. They would be ably assisted by the economic hitmen of the International Monetary Fund and World Bank.

The resulting chaos, bloodshed, secessions, coups d'etat, military dictatorships and subsequent collapse in health and living standards would be deemed as regrettable, but unavoidable consequences. Only Portugal, Rhodesia and South Africa were prepared to resist this lunacy. In the first half of 1960 South Africa was subjected to a three pronged attack – the visit of British Prime Minister, Harold Macmillan, followed by the CIA-orchestrated riots at Sharpeville and in other urban areas, and the MI6 planned assassination of Dr. Verwoerd. All three events were intended to prepare the ground for a violent revolution, which ultimately failed.

---

108 J. Botha, *op.cit.*, 73. It may be noted that agitation for a republic was confined not only to Afrikaans-speaking South Africans. See J.J. McCord, *South African Struggle*, J.H. De Busssy, Pretoria, 1952, where the author Captain John James McCord postulates that unity of the White races is vital, if they are to survive as a nation. Chapter XXVII is titled, A Republic is essential for unity.

Harold Macmillan's Visit

On 5 January 1960 Harold Macmillan accompanied by his wife Lady Dorothy departed on his errand to inform the various colonial administrations that their time was up. On 27 January 1960 the Macmillans arrived in Johannesburg. While Mr. Macmillan was in Pretoria he visited the African township of Meadowlands and Pietersburg in the Northern Transvaal. At the latter venue he met Chief Frank Maserumule who gave Mr. Macmillan a leopard skin which he draped over his shoulders. Chief Chuene then informed Mr. Macmillan: "You see for yourself now – we do not live in chains!"[109]

British prime minister, Harold Macmillan & Dr. Verwoerd at Groote Schuur. Cape Town, February 1960. A consensus could not be reached as Macmillan was obsessed with the false notion that African people were clamouring for "independence".

On 1 February 1960 the Macmillans arrived in Cape Town and stayed at the prime minister's residence, Groote Schuur. The following morning the two prime ministers had a discussion lasting several hours.[110] Dr. Verwoerd soon realised that he could not have any confidence in Mr. Macmillan and viewed him with suspicion. He was shocked to learn that he was not a man of principle when he said that a leader must not be narrow-minded, and should be able to adjust his principles as a boat adjusts its sails to the wind".[111]

The following morning at 10.30 am Mr. Macmillan gave his famous "wind of change" speech. Ironically, during his stay in Cape Town there was a strong south-easter wind and the top of Table Mountain was covered in white cloud. It is a British parliamentary convention that the prime minister makes available a copy of his speech to his opposite number. Dr. Verwoerd's secretary, Fred

---
109 *Verwoerd aan die Woord*, op.cit., 317.
110 F. Barnard, *op.cit.*, 70. Immediately after the meeting Dr. Verwoerd went to his study and wrote up a complete summary of what had been discussed – something which he had never done previously.
111 *Verwoerd aan die Woord*, op.cit., 524.

Barnard, patiently waited to receive it, but it never came,[112] even though embargoed copies had already been distributed to the press. This was a sly trick, not unknown to British politicians, whereby Mr. Macmillan hoped to cause Dr. Verwoerd maximum discomfit and embarrassment by catching him on the back foot.

Mr. Macmillan's speech consisted of ten typed pages, which had been prepared months before in Whitehall, and was delivered in what is usually known as diplomatic "speak" as he condemned and insulted his host in guarded language,[113] warning White South Africans that they should mend their ways and fit in with what was happening elsewhere in Africa. Mr. Macmillan droned on sonorously about the fact that:

"The most striking of all the impressions I have formed since I left London a month ago is of the strength of this African national consciousness. In different places it takes different forms, but it is happening everywhere. The wind of change is blowing throughout the continent...

He continued:

"As I see it, the great issue in this second half of the twentieth century is whether the uncommitted peoples of Asia and Africa will swing to the East or the West...

"Of course, I realise that these are hard, difficult and sometimes baffling problems...As a fellow member of the Commonwealth we have always tried to give South Africa our support and encouragement, but I hope you will not mind my saying frankly that there are some aspects of your policies which make it impossible for us to do this without being false to our own deep convictions about the political destinies of free men to which in our own territories we are trying to give effect".[114]

This was a fine example of British hypocrisy,[115] as we now know this "wind of change" was not intended to liberate the Black people, but to replace one form of control which was honest and direct, with another form of white power exercised indirectly and dishonestly through puppet regimes no matter how brutal and inefficient.

---

112 F. Barnard, *op.cit.*, 71-72.
113 *Ibid.*, 72.
114 J. Botha, *op.cit.*, 55, The term "Wind of Change" was conceived by James Robertson, a Principal in the Colonial Office attached to Harold Macmillan for his tour of Africa.
115 A typical example of British hypocrisy occurred in 1965 when the Ford Motor Co. of Canada received an order from the South African government to purchase 9,000 6x6 2½ ton trucks, which was its largest off shore sale in its history. The British Foreign Office admonished the Canadian High Commissioner in London and advised him to cancel the sale as it would reflect badly on Canada's reputation, which would be seen as a supporter of the "detestable, racist" regime. The External Affairs department put pressure on the Ford Motor Co. to cancel the order which they reluctantly did, at the same time deeply offending the South African government and forestalling any future sales. Six months later Bedford Trucks, a division of General Motors United Kingdom, received a similar order from the "detestable, racist" regime which was gratefully accepted and approved by the British government. Information supplied to the author by retired Canadian diplomat, Ian V. Macdonald, 455 Wilbrod Street, Ottawa ON K1N 6M7. See also Canadian trucks for Communist China? Certainly. Canadian Trucks for South Africa? Certainly not!, *The South African Observer*, February 1966, 15.

Dr. Verwoerd who never used notes and was able to speak coherently and intelligently for hours on end (his longest speech was for three hours in the Senate) had no difficulty in countering Mr. Macmillan's fallacious arguments, as the following extract shows:

"We call ourselves European, but actually we represent the White man of Africa. They are the only people, not only in the Union, but through major portions of Africa, who brought civilisation here, who made the development of Black nationalism possible, to bring them education, by showing them this way of life, by bringing them industrial development, by bringing them the ideals which Western civilisation has developed itself.

"And the White man who came to Africa perhaps to trade in some cases, perhaps to bring the gospel, has remained to stay and particularly we in the southernmost portion of Africa have such a stake here that this is our only motherland; we have nowhere else to go. We settled a country bare and the Bantu came in this country and settled certain portions for themselves and it is in line with the thinking of Africa to grant those fullest rights which we also, with you, admit all people should have. We believe in providing those rights for those people in the fullest degree in that part of Southern Africa which their forefathers found for themselves and settled in, but similarly we believe in balance. We believe in allowing exactly those same full opportunities to remain within the grasp of the White man who has made this all possible, and we also see ourselves as a part of the western world, a true White state in Africa, with the possibility of granting a full future to the Black man in our midst".[116]

The press asked for copies of Dr. Verwoerd's impressive riposte, but none were available. Copies were later printed and were still being sought years after the event.

Dr. Verwoerd was very strict about not criticising the internal affairs of other countries, but after the British ambassador, Sir John Maud, had tried to interfere in the administration of South African justice, he made an exception and deviated from this policy when he told the British with great relevance and foresight:

"Britain should be careful about the immigration of non-Whites on such a large scale; Britain was a proud nation who had rendered great services to the world, but if Britain wanted to remain proud of its nationhood it should stop allowing non-Whites in by the thousand; they were making a bastard race of themselves and this would one day be the source of many difficulties for the British people".[117]

---

[116] Botha, *op.cit.*, 56.
[117] *Ibid.*, 114.

SHARPEVILLE RIOT

On Monday, 21 March 1960 a nation-wide anti-pass campaign began under the auspices of the Pan African Congress. Lurking behind the scenes was a CIA front, the African American Institute,[118] whose *agents provocateurs* had intimidated Black workers and dragged them out of their homes in order to enforce their participation.[119] They also prevented all the bus drivers from taking the workers to their places of employment. Another key figure who stoked up the agitation was the Bishop of Johannesburg, Bishop Ambrose Reeves,[120] who fled the country shortly thereafter on 1 April 1960 as "a persecuted Christian".[121] There were no grounds for any form of resentment. As has already been pointed out, the principal purpose of the passes was to protect existing workers from the influx of non-urban Blacks and illegal immigrants, who would force wages down and reduce their living standards. Workers were being housed in huge new townships and Black unemployment was low at about 10%.[122]

The major flashpoint was a police station at Sharpeville, Vereeniging where 20,000 Blacks armed with pangas (machetes), metal pipes and guns were demanding that they be arrested for having destroyed their passes. Reinforcements could not be summoned as the telephone wires had been cut ahead of time by the revolutionaries. 150 policemen were trying to calm the crowd down, when a constable's revolver accidentally fell out of his holster and discharged a shot. The crowd then advanced. With the memory of the Cato Manor riot in Durban, which had happened only two months previously on 24 January 1960, when four white and five Black policemen were hacked to death, they opened fire on the menacing crowd. 69 were killed and 180 were wounded.

---

118 P.J. Pretorius, op.cit., 134. See also P. C. Swanepoel, *Really Inside BOSS A Tale of South Africa's late Intelligence Service (And Something about the CIA)*, Self-published, Pretoria, 2008, 125, where the writer confirms that the African American Institute was a front financed by the CIA, and A. Parker, Secret US War on South Africa, *The Citizen*, Johannesburg, 1977, 10. In his biography Prince Mangosuthu Buthelezi reveals that the Institute sponsored his visit to East Africa in November 1973. B. Temkin, *Buthelezi A Biography*, Frank Cass & Co. Ltd, London, 2003, 164.
119 J. Botha, *op.cit.*, 58.
120 J.A. Marais, *op.cit.*, 113. Marais cites an extract from *Faith under Fire* by Canon L. John Collins, where at a meeting convened by Bishop Reeves, 39 out of 40 Anglican priests present, produced an ANC membership card.
121 *Ibid.*, 114.
122 *Ibid.*, 23-24.

Weapons, which included guns, metal pipes and machetes, recovered after the CIA instigated riot at Sharpeville police station, southern Transvaal in March 1960. In present day South African school history books, it is claimed that there were only 4,000 protestors (when there were in fact 20,000) and that they were "friendly and unarmed".

Sensational reports were spread by journalists and photographers who seemingly had already positioned themselves before the event.[123] The Security Council of the United Nations convened to discuss a potential threat to international peace and security. The United States sent a note "deploring"[124] what had happened and blamed Dr. Verwoerd. At a meeting held in Meyerton, Transvaal on 26 March 1960 attended by 80,000 supporters, Dr. Verwoerd informed them that *"Ons is bewus daarvan dat agter heelwat van die opstokery wit kragte sit"* (We are aware that behind much of the agitation there are white powers).[125] The conclusion reached by former National Intelligence Services officer, Advocate Piet Pretorius, was that the Sharpeville incident was a false flag operation, engineered by the CIA.[126] On 31 August 1960 the state of emergency was lifted.

---

123 *Ibid.*, 104.
124 *Ibid.*, 104.
125 *Verwoerd aan die Woord, op.cit.*, 356.
126 P.J. Pretorius, *op.cit.*, 134.

First Assassination Attempt

Prior to the first assassination attempt on Dr. Verwoerd on 9 April 1960 at the Union Exposition held at the Witwatersrand Show Grounds by a disturbed multi-millionaire, David Beresford Pratt, the leading business organisations in South Africa took it upon themselves to demand various fundamental changes in government policy. The Association of Chambers of Commerce, South African Federated Chamber of Industries, Chamber of Mines and the Afrikaanse Handelsinstituut said that grievances of the Blacks must be removed, there must be no penalties for disobeying the pass system, the liquor laws must be changed, wages must be raised, the Blacks must no longer be treated as migrant labour, but as permanent residents with property rights and representation in local[127] government and that the homelands must be developed with white capital. Adding to this crescendo for a complete reversal of National Party policy was Margaret Ballinger, one of the three former Native representatives in parliament,[128] who launched a campaign on 27 March 1960 under the slogan "Verwoerd must go".

Shortly after Dr. Verwoerd had given the opening address that afternoon, while he was seated, he was approched by Pratt who fired two shots from a 22 pistol at point-blank range. The first bullet penetrated Dr. Verwoerd's right cheek near his nostril just below his skull. By a miracle it missed all his vital structures such as the spinal cord, carotid artery, jugular vein, vagus nerve, thyroid and respiratory passage. A second bullet struck him just below the ear, while a third shot went off as Pratt was being overpowered by bystanders. Dr. Verwoerd was taken in a conscious state to the Johannesburg General Hospital, where shortly after his admission a number of Jewish surgeons offered their "services", which were politely refused. Two days later he was transferred to the Pretoria General Hospital. While in hospital Dr. Verwoerd received messages of sympathy from all races and groups, including one from The Queen.[129] In the words of one of the specialists, Dr. Verwoerd's recovery was "absolutely miraculous"[130] and on 15 May 1960 he returned to his official home Libertas. On 31 May 1960 he gave a speech at the Union Festival in Bloemfontein, which commemorated the first 50 years of the Union of South Africa.

Pratt, who had been suffering for years from fits of epilepsy and depression, appeared before a preliminary hearing in the Johannesburg Magistrates' Court on 20 and 21 July 1960. Medical reports filed by five different psychiatrists confirmed that Pratt could not be held criminally liable for having shot Dr.

---
127 J.A. Marais, *op.cit.*, 105-106.
128 *Ibid.*, 106.
129 "I was shocked to learn of the attack on your life and I hope you will make a speedy recovery". G.Allighan, *op.cit.*, xxiii.
130 J. Botha, *op.cit.*, 65.

Verwoerd and on 20 September 1960 he was committed to the Oranje Hospital for mental patients in Bloemfontein. Both Advocate Piet Pretorius[131] and Jaap Marais[132] have expressed the opinion that MI6 was behind Dr. Verwoerd's attempted assassination. However, the most compelling evidence supporting this thesis has been provided by Dr. Allan Bird in his book *Bird on the wing: Autobiography, 1916-1992*. Allan Bird practised as a neurologist in Johannesburg. In 1953 Dr. Solly Jacobson, who had studied medicine at the universities of the Witwatersrand, Edinburgh and London joined his practice. Jacobson was deeply involved in the politics of the South African Communist Party and one of his "closest friends"[133] was its secretary general, Joe Slovo (real name Yossel Mashel Slovotnik). Bird attended several, clandestine gatherings meeting both Slovo and Mandela, but later lost interest, as he did not like the subversive nature of these meetings. On one occasion in 1959 Jacobson blurted out: "If Verwoerd goes on like this HE IS GOING TO GET A BULLET" adding that "Verwoerd is a mad man and is dragging the country to ruin".[134]

On the night of the assassination, Jacobson telephoned his colleague Bird in a highly agitated state and asked him to visit his patient, David Pratt, at the Police Forensic Laboratory in Braamfontein, where he was being examined. Jacobson was afraid that Pratt might be tortured and reveal who had been handling him. Advocate Israel "Issy" Maisels,[135] a close associate of Jacobson, also came on the line and pleaded with Bird to go there, but Bird refused saying that Pratt was not his patient. As it transpired nothing untoward happened to Pratt and he was treated very kindly.[136]

On 1 October 1961 Pratt committed suicide. Jacobson was inconsolable with grief. Bird then came to the startling conclusion that Jacobson had coached the unstable and drug dependent Pratt to murder Dr. Verwoerd. Bird writes as follows:

"As I was trying to console Solly, he told me that Pratt's original suicide attempt was brought about by Verwoerd's plans to impose apartheid

---

131 P.J. Pretorius, *op.cit.*, 135.
132 J.A. Marais, *op.cit.*, 114.
133 A. Bird, *Bird on the wing: Autobiography, 1916-1992*, South African Natural History Publications, Johannesburg, 1992, 203.
134 *Ibid.*, 204.
135 I. Benson, *Truth Out Of Africa Lessons for all Nations*, Veritas Publishing Company (Pty) Ltd, Cranbrook, Western Australia, 1995, xii. Ivor Benson quotes from Dr. Gideon Shimoni's *Jews and Zionism: the South African Experience 1910-1967*, Oxford University Press, Cape Town, 1980 as follows; "To top it all at one stage (in the great Treason Trial which began in December 1956), the defence counsel was led by Israel Maisels…Maisels, the prominent Jewish communal leader, defending those accused of seeking to overthrow White supremacy".
136 A. Bird, *op.cit.*, 207-208.

through Parliament. But after treatment with psychotherapy and anti depressant drugs, Pratt began to think more logically, Jacobson pointed out to him that, if he had died from overdose, he would have achieved nothing towards curtailing apartheid. I gathered that between them they worked out a plan to shoot Verwoerd. As he suffered from epilepsy, according to the Mental Disorders Act of 1916, he was insane and would not have to stand trial."[137]

According to Gordon Winter, an informer of South Africa's secret police (1963-1979), who fled to Ireland and wrote a controversial book *Inside B.O.S.S.: South Africa's Secret Police*, the trigger image which Jacobson brainwashed Pratt with was a black bull. When Pratt saw a black bull in the show ring, he was prompted to shoot Dr. Verwoerd at close range.[138]

Minister of External Affairs, Eric Louw, and Dr. Verwoerd on their way to a meeting of the Commonwealth prime ministers in London, March 1961.

COMMONWEALTH CONFERENCE

From 8 to 17 March 1961 Dr. Verwoerd attended the Commonwealth Conference at Lancaster House, London with his Minister of External Affairs, Eric Louw. At the time of the referendum Dr. Verwoerd had given the assurance that he would seek to maintain South Africa's membership of that body. However,

---
137 *Ibid.*, 209.
138 http://etd.uwc.ac.za/xmlui/bitstream/handle/11394/2912/Adams_PHD_2011.PDF?sequence =1 In the documentary The Afrikanerbond https://www.youtube.com/watch?v=9XG3FcP_NG0&app= desktop at 9 minutes 9 seconds the black bull, which was the trigger symbol can be seen near Dr. Verwoerd in the show ring, prior to his attempted assassination.

because there was a proposed change in South Africa's constitutional status from a dominion to a republic, South Africa would have to make an application to have its membership renewed. Although it was not the custom to deliberate on the internal affairs of member states, Dr. Verwoerd gave permission for South Africa's policies to be discussed. With the exception of the prime ministers of Australia and New Zealand, Robert Menzies[139] and Keith Holyoake respectively, the attitude of the rest of the leaders was very unfriendly, if not outright inimical, in particular Kwame Nkrumah of Ghana and John Diefenbaker of Canada. The incongruity was that all these countries practised discrimination in one form or another, and some of them were not even democracies.

Australia had a White Australia Policy of immigration since its founding in 1901 and practised apartheid in Papua Guinea. In Canada the indigenous inhabitants, the Eskimos (Inuit) and Red Indian tribes did not have the vote, while since 1876 tens of thousands of aboriginal children had been kidnapped and forced to live in White communities and attend White schools.[140] Ceylon subjugated its Tamil minority in the north of the island. Ghana was a dictatorship whose leader of the opposition had recently fled to Holland, while most of the opposition members were in prison, some of whom had been sentenced to flogging. India had a caste (colour) system in which 85% of the population, the Harijan or Dalits, were deemed to be untouchable and severely discriminated against. Malaya oppressed its Chinese minority to such an extent that there were serious riots in 1964 which a year later led to Singapore forming its own state. Nigeria was a cauldron of discontent with the Igbos in the south resenting the Hausa in the north. In less than four years there was a coup d'etat in which its leader, Sir Abubakar Tafawa Balewa was murdered and found lying in a ditch. Pakistan was a military dictatorship.

Dr. Verwoerd explained South Africa's policies eloquently and as usual without notes, which enabled him to respond to those who had spoken before him. Although he did not appear to be making much impact, he still held the belief that South Africa would retain its membership of the Commonwealth up until the last day. During the afternoon of 15 March 1961 the text of the final communiqué was discussed. The principal impediment was the inclusion of a statement that condemned South Africa's domestic policies and which would be repeated at all future conferences. This meant that members would reserve the right to introduce a motion to expel South Africa at any time in the future and some members such as Ghana, indicated that they would reserve the right to retain their membership, while South Africa was still a member.

---

139 J. Botha, *op.cit.*, 83. On his return home, Robert Menzies said that: "I would have withdrawn the application if I had been in his place". He also said that he would not have tolerated interference in Australia's [White] immigration policy.

140 J. Barber, Canada's indigenous schools policy was 'cultural genocide', says report, *The Guardian*, 2 June 2015. 150,000 or 30% of all aboriginal children were placed in Christian schools, where they were forced to abandon their language and native culture.

At 5.20 pm Dr. Verwoerd addressed the conference as follows:

"South Africa is one of the senior members of the Commonwealth and has in the past heartily co-operated with its fellow members. No self-respecting member of any voluntary organisation could, however, in view of what is being suggested and the degree of interference shown with what are South Africa's domestic affairs, be expected to wish to retain membership in what is now becoming a pressure group. Under the circumstances I wish formally to withdraw my request for South Africa to remain a member of the Commonwealth after she becomes a republic on May 31st".[141]

Dr. Verwoerd went on to say:

"I do, however, wish to state that it is ironical that those allegations have come from Prime Ministers in whose countries oppression and discrimination are openly practised and where the basic principles of democratic government are flouted. In this connection I refer in particular to Ghana, India, Malaya and Ceylon, although certain other Commonwealth countries are also not free from such practices which are sanctioned by legal enactments".[142] Dr. Verwoerd also found the attitude of Canada immature – "if you find a group of nations which cannot come together and forget their differences, then I think you are acting like a child".[143]

In his closing words Dr. Verwoerd said that:

"The practices which have led to the present unsatisfactory conditions prevailing in the United Nations will, I venture to predict, lead to the eventual disintegration of the Commonwealth, which all would regret".[144]

By withdrawing South Africa's application, Dr. Verwoerd took the only statesmanlike option open to him, and when he returned to South Africa he received a tumultuous welcome from a crowd of over 50,000 supporters at Jan Smuts airport, Johannesburg.

---

[141] *Verwoerd aan die Woord, op.cit.*, 503.
[142] *Ibid.*, 504.
[143] J. Botha, *op.cit.*, 82.
[144] *Verwoerd aan die Woord, op.cit.*, 504.

Visit of Dag Hammarskjöld

From 6 -12 January 1961 the Secretary General of the United Nations, Dag Hammarskjöld visited Dr. Verwoerd for extended discussions. The talks lasted six days and included a visit to the Transkei. Mr. Hammarskjöld was very impressed by the honest and positive steps which Dr. Verwoerd was taking in order to resolve South Africa's racial relationships.[145] From a South African point of view the visit was deemed to have been a great success. A second visit was scheduled to take place, but Mr. Hammarskjöld was killed in a mysterious airplane crash[146] near Ndola, Northern Rhodesia on 18 September 1961. When he died, Dr. Verwoerd recalled that Mr. Hammarskjöld had "grasped the position in this country" and that "he had not been afraid of the truth". He lamented the fact that South Africa "had lost a friend".[147]

Dr. Verwoerd and the Secretary General of the United Nations, Dag Hammarskjold. Both parties engaged in positive discussions with Mr. Hammarskjold exhibiting sympathy and understanding towards South Africa's policy of separate development.

Early in February 1961 a naïve and irresponsible Swedish authoress, Sara

---

145 F. Barnard, *op.cit.*, 154.
146 G. Björkdahl, 'I have no doubt Dag Hammarskjöld's plane was brought down', *The Guardian*, 17 August 2011. The writer is of the opinion that the connections of the Belgian mining house, Union Minière, wished to protect their investments by allowing the mineral rich Katanga province to secede from the Congo, in contravention of the United Nations mandate to end the secession. Hammarskjold had a hole in his head and there is a supposition that he may have survived the crash, but been assassinated by a member of the Northern Rhodesian police. A motive for the murder may be that a rival organisation, Liberian American Swedish Minerals Company, one of whose key members was Bo Hammarskjold, Dag Hammarskjold's brother, wished to exploit Katanga's mineral resources at the expense of Union Minière. See A.K. Chesterton, *The New Unhappy Lords*, Candour Publishing Co. Liss Forest, Hampshire, 1975, Chapter XV U.N. Ideals and the Reality, 111-119.
147 S.E.D. Brown, Nordic Countries 'Afraid To See The Truth about S.A.', says Verwoerd, *The South African Observer*, October 1963, 16.

Lidman, was arrested together with Peter Nthite, the National Organising Secretary of the African National Congress at her flat in Johannesburg for having transgressed the Immorality Act. After Mr. Hammarskjöld contacted Dr. Verwoerd, the charges were dropped and she left South Africa.[148]

FIELD MARSHAL VISCOUNT BERNARD LAW MONTGOMERY OF ALAMEIN

In November and December 1947 Field Marshal Montgomery, who was at that time Chief of the Imperial General Staff, visited eleven African countries. Thereafter he produced a top secret master plan based on the injection of large numbers of White men with brains who would develop these colonies and which would act as a bulwark against communism. These territories would also be aligned with the Union of South Africa. In his report he said that "There will be many people in the UK who will oppose such a plan on the grounds that the African will suffer in the process; there is no reason why he should suffer, and in any case he is a complete savage and is quite incapable of developing the country himself ". Montgomery's plan was rejected by the Labour government, who had their own plans for selling out these territories to the international bankers. In his response Montgomery said "It is obvious we disagree ... Time will tell which of us was right".[149]

In November 1959 Field Marshal Montgomery visited South Africa as a private citizen for two weeks. He said that the purpose of his visit was "to give the lie to a great many things which are being said about what is going on in this country".[150] On 26 November 1959, accompanied by his wartime chief of staff, Major General Sir Francis de Guingand, Montgomery had a two hour conversation with Dr. Verwoerd in Pretoria. Afterwards he said that the meeting had been a "pleasant surprise... this obviously sincere, quiet-spoken and kindly man. He impressed me as a leader, a man of decision and action".[151] Before sailing for England he said that "he had the greatest admiration for Dr. Verwoerd".[152] There were further visits by Field Marshal Montgomery in June 1961 and in 1962 when a dinner, which included 28 guests, was held in his honour at Dr. Verwoerd's Cape Town residence, Groote Schuur, on 25 January 1962 and on 13 February 1963 when Montgomery had tea with Dr. Verwoerd.[153]

---

148 Early in February 1961 a naïve and foolish Swedish authoress, Sara Lidman, was arrested together with Peter Nthite, the National Organising Secretary of the African National Congress at her flat in Johannesburg for having transgressed the Immorality Act. After Mr. Hammarskjöld contacted Dr. Verwoerd, the charges were dropped and she left South Africa. F. Hale The South African Immorality Act and Sara Lidman's *Jag och min son? (My son and I?)* http://www.scriptageologica.nl/cgi/t/text/get-pdf?c=tvs;idno=2101a04. See also *Verwoerd só onthou ons hom, op.cit.*, B. Fourie, Buitelandse Sake Onder Dr. Verwoerd, 128.
149 B.L. Montgomery, *The Memoirs of Field-Marshal Montgomery*, Collins, London, 1958, 462-465.
150 J. Botha, *op.cit.*, 122.
151 *Ibid.*, 122.
152 S.E.D. Brown, Montgomery To Be Guest Of Verwoerd, *The South African Observer*, October 1963, 16.
153 A. Boshoff, *Sekretaresse vir die Verwoerds*, Human & Rousseau, Kaapstad, 1974, 80.

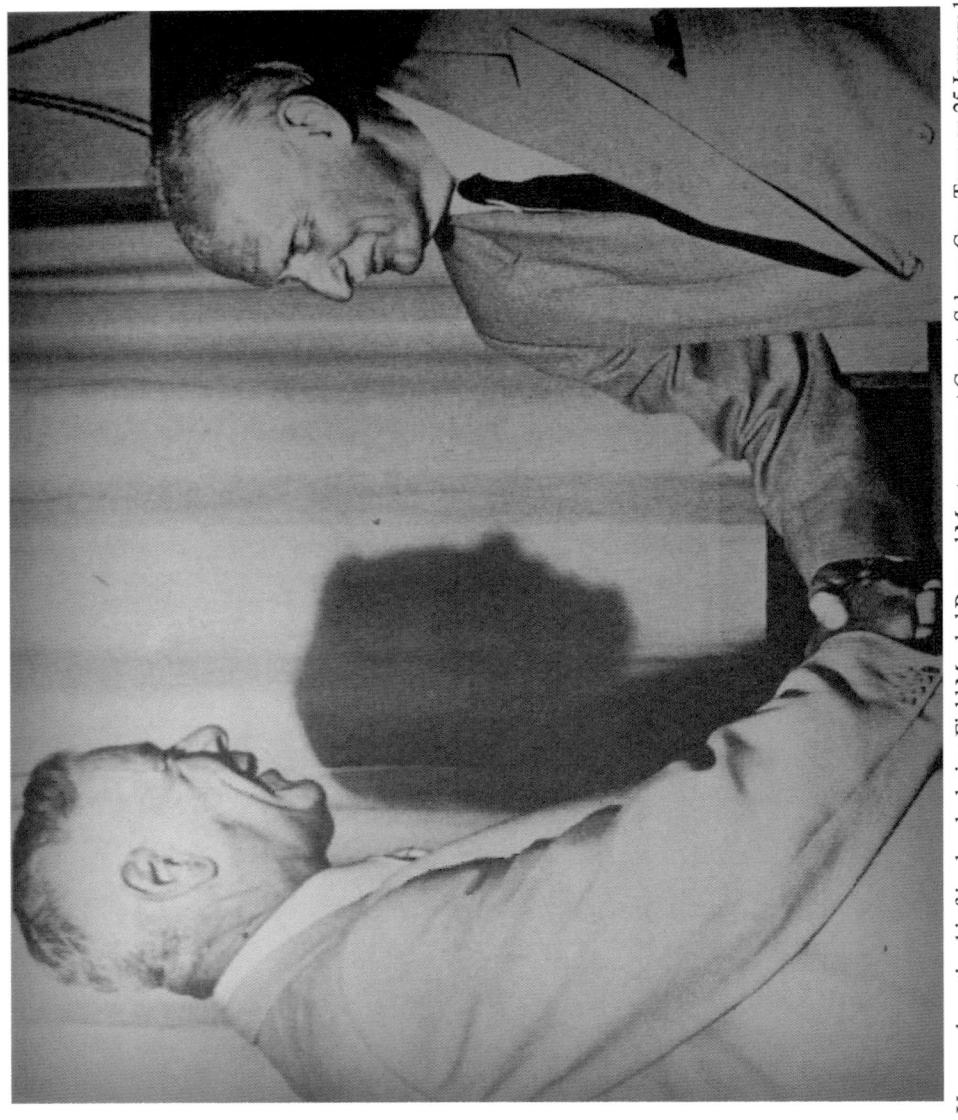

Dr. Verwoerd greeting his friend and admirer Field Marshal Bernard Montgomery at Groote Schuur, Cape Town on 25 January 1962.

Clash with the Jews

On 11 October 1961 at the United Nations, Israel cast a vote of censure against Foreign Minister Eric Louw's speech, in which he had defended South Africa's policy of separate development. In reply to a letter received from a Jewish professional man, Mr. A.S.A. East, who tried to justify Israel's vote against South Africa, Dr. Verwoerd replied that South Africa had always "had a feeling of sympathy for Israel and general preparedness to co-operate was noticeable in South Africa amongst all sections". He was irked, if not betrayed, by the hypocrisy of Israel and raised the rhetorical question as to "why, if Israel and its Rabbis feel impelled to attack the policy of separate development here, the policy of separate development of Israel is not wrong in their eyes as well.[154] He said that it was "a tragedy for Jewry in South Africa" and drew attention to the fact that so many Jews had voted for the Progressive Party and not for the National Party in the recent general election. He also said that South Africa did not want "to oppress, but that it is correct that we wish to differentiate and separate where there are fundamental differences, whether they are symbolised by colour or not. For that reason we believed in the separate State of Israel, but now begin to wonder whether that support should be withdrawn if, according to their own convictions, the ideal of separate development is fundamentally wrong".[155]

Without obtaining Dr. Verwoerd's permission this private correspondence was revealed in the press and produced a strong reaction. However, Dr. Verwoerd was unmoved and at a conference of the National Party Witwatersrand Executive he defended his point of view when he asked "What is the value of the so called threat in the letter? If I want to threaten the Jews of South Africa, I will threaten the whole lot of them".[156]

The following year when Israel again voted against South Africa's domestic policies at the United Nations, the South African Jewish Board of Deputies immediately issued a statement deploring Israel's stand and affirming its loyalty to South Africa.

In August 1966 a delegation of Jews had an appointment with Dr. Verwoerd. They appeared to be quite animated. However, the conversation did not last long and a somewhat dejected group exited Dr Verwoerd's office after they had seemingly failed in their objective to persuade Dr. Verwoerd to change his policies.[157]

---
154 S.E.D. Brown, Verwoerd Letter Causes Stir In Israel and S.A., *The South African Observer*, December 1961, 16.
155 *Ibid.*, 16.
156 B. Bunting, *The Rise of the South African Reich*, Penguin Books Ltd, London, 1969, 43-44.
157 J.A. Marais, *op.cit.*, 176.

Transkei

In January 1962 Dr. Verwoerd announced at the opening of parliament that the Transkei, a territory of 43,798 km² (16,911 sq mi) in the north east of the Cape Province, would attain self-government the following year. (Independence would follow 13 years later in 1976). Chief Kaiser Matanzima, chairman of the Transkeian Territorial Authority, declared: "To the people of the Transkei, wherever they are, the Prime Minister's statement is highly welcomed and will be received with excitement. It is significant of the policy enunciated 13 years ago, and the stage has been attained, and reflects the honesty of the Government".[158] He said that he had already won back many ex-antagonists to the system of Bantu self-government. For the White liberals, Chief Matanzima had nothing but disdain, stating that: "The White liberals are not sincere. They are there to mislead us, with the purpose of keeping us down so that we will never rise".[159]

On 18 January 1963 Chief Matanzima was interviewed by Independent Television for the programme *Roving Report*. He informed the British television audience that apartheid was "the best solution for the whole world". He referred to racial conflict between Black and White in Britain, the United States and Southern Rhodesia and said that : "This shows that if people can be kept separate and have their own administrations, the relationship will be better".[160] He denied that he was a stooge of the White man and said that "the majority of Africans in South Africa supported his policy ". He was full of praise for Dr. Verwoerd and described him as "the greatest leader who has emerged among White South Africans".[161]

German South West Africa

Since 1884 South West Africa had been ruled by Imperial Germany, which had the distinction of being one of the ablest and fairest colonial administrators in Africa.[162]

On 31 August 1914 almost four weeks after Great Britain had declared war on Germany, Brigadier General Tim Lukin landed at Port Nolloth, situated in the north western corner of South Africa, with 2,420 soldiers. They proceeded to Steinkopf on the border with German South West Africa and waited for Generals Botha and Smuts to give the signal to commence the invasion. On

---
158 S.E.D. Brown, "A Day Of Jubilation," Says Transkei Chief, *The South African Observer,* February 1962, 7.
159 *Ibid.*, 7.
160 S.E.D. Brown, Apartheid 'The Best Solution', Says Transkei Chief, *The South African Observer*, February 1963, 15.
161 *Ibid.*, 15.
162 C. Nordbruch, Genocide of the Hereros? Black tribe in Namibia demands German reparations for what respected author says is non-existent genocide, *The Barnes Review,* Vol. XVIII No. 6, Washington, D.C., November/December 2012, 22-32.

the night of 14- 15 September Smuts, who was Minister of Defence gave the signal and Lieutenant Colonel F.S. Dawson with the 4th South African Mounted Rifles crossed the Orange River at Raman's Drift and engaged the Germans stationed there. General Lukin crossed the Orange River at the same place with the rest of the invading force of volunteers.[163] The primary purpose of the invading army was not to seize the powerful wireless transmitters at Lüderitzbucht and Swakopmund, but to secure the diamond fields along the southern coast for Ernest Oppenheimer, who was the principal representative in South Africa of the Rothschild banking group.[164]

On 9 July 1915 the South African expeditionary force of 67,000 soldiers, under the command of General Louis Botha, defeated the much smaller German army of 8,000 soldiers, including 3,000 *schutztruppe* (protection force), led by General Victor Franke.

SOUTH WEST AFRICA

On 28 June 1919 at the Peace Conference at Versailles, South Africa was awarded South West Africa as a class C mandate. This allowed the territory to be administered under the laws of the Mandatory as an integral part of its own territory. Since the granting of the mandate, South West Africa was ruled as a fifth province of South Africa. From 1950 white voters were represented by four members of parliament and six senators in the South African parliament.

The League of Nations dissolved itself on 18 April 1946. South Africa did not recognise any United Nations jurisdiction and refused to place the territory under the latter's trusteeship and thus continued to rule it under the terms of its League of Nations mandate. This decision was endorsed by a referendum held during May and June of the same year when 208,850 or 85.5% of the tribal population in a voter turnout of 242,370 or 81.1% of the eligible voters, voted in favour of becoming part of South Africa.[165]

Over the following years committees of the United Nations drew up numerous reports containing accusations of racial discrimination, oppression, militarisation of the territory and genocide. There were also demands that its inhabitants be granted self-determination. All these reports and demands for information and particulars about the administration of South West Africa were ignored.

---

163 L. J. Bothma, *Rebelspoor: Die aanloop, verloop en afloop van die Boereopstand van 1914-15*, Self-published, Langenhovenpark, Orange Free State, 2015, 169-170.
164 *Ibid.*, 403, 410-411.
165 J. Botha, *op.cit.*, 231. See also South West Africa: A Case Reviewed, *CODICILLVS*, Faculty of Law, University of South Africa, Special Edition, October 1966, 36.

The indigenous population and its leaders were strongly in favour of continued White rule. While he was Minister of Bantu Affairs, Dr. Verwoerd visited the territory. He was welcomed by a crowd of over 20,000[166] many of whom had travelled on foot to see in person the man whom they believed would be capable of providing them all with a better life.[167] One of the main leaders of the Ovambo people, Ananias Shapeka, who had been a member of Windhoek's Non-European Advisory Council since 1933 and who was considered to be the "father" of the detribalised Ovambos, believed implicitly in separate development of the different racial groups. He said that: "God has made us separate entities, not the Government, and for that reason, it must stay like that. We do not wish to intermarry with Europeans. That is a sin".[168] He also warned that if South West Africa became independent the tribes would exterminate each other as in pre-colonial times, as the Non-European tribes despised each other. He had nothing but contempt for the future puppet leader of Namibia, Sam Nujoma, describing him as a child and a "little upstart". [169]

A half-brother of the Chief of the Hereros Hosea Kutako, Aaron Mungunda, who considered himself to be the real leader of the Hereros and had also been a member of the Non-European Advisory Board since 1925, expressed similar sentiments, saying that only White rule prevented bloodletting. He said that the Black man in South Africa had developed more than in any other country in Africa, "and even overseas" and wanted to know "In what other country is the Black man better off than here?"[170] As far as the pass laws were concerned, he felt that they should not be abolished under any circumstances and said that he himself carried a pass, which he looked upon as an "identity certificate".

Richard Forster, the leader of the Griquas, declared that "It is surprising to hear people still speak of oppression of the non-Whites in South West Africa. The non-Whites have made such rapid progress that they already use English as their first language in the street".[171]

---

166 At that time South West Africa had a population of 1,000,000. Thus 20,000 would have represented 7.5% of the adult male Black population.
167 J.J.J. Scholtz, *Die Moord op Dr Verwoerd*, Nasionale Boekhandel Bpk, 1967, 79.
168 S.E.D. Brown, An Independent S.W.A. "Would Become Second Congo" Says Ovambo Leader, *The South African Observer*, May 1962, 13-14.
169 *Ibid.*, 14. In 2015 28.7% of the population was living in poverty, while the official unemployment rate was recorded at 29.9%, although unofficially it is believed to be as high as 50%. http://www.na.undp.org/content/namibia/en/home/library/poverty/nimdpovmao2015.html In 2013 the Gini Co-efficient, which measures the distribution of income among individuals, stood at 63.9, one of the highest and worst in the world.
170 S.E.D. Brown, Presence Of Whites In S.W.A Prevents Conflicts, Says Herero, *The South African Observer,* May 1962, 13.
171 S.E.D. Brown, Apartheid In S.W.A. "Is Just", Chief Tells U.N., *The South African Observer*, April 1963, 11.

In June 1958, notwithstanding the fact that the United Nations had no custodial function over the mandate, the South African government permitted a delegation of the General Assembly's SWA committee under the chairmanship of Sir Charles Arden-Clarke, a former governor of Nigeria, to visit the territory. The delegation toured South West Africa extensively and had discussions with Dr. Verwoerd. They were very impressed with what was being undertaken and reported that there were no signs of the serious allegations, such as the existence of military bases, which had been made against South Africa. The fourth committee of the General Assembly was so enraged with the favourable report of the Arden-Clarke committee that it was immediately disbanded and nothing further was heard of its positive findings.[172]

In May 1962 in a master stroke of diplomacy, Dr. Verwoerd granted a two man United Nations special committee on South West Africa permission to visit the territory. No restrictions were placed on their movements and on the people they wished to meet. The chairman and vice-chairman were Dr. Vittorio Carpio of the Philippines and Dr. Salvador Martinez de Alva of Mexico respectively. Prior to the completion of their ten day mission the two United Nations' representatives had a meeting with Dr. Verwoerd in Pretoria, after which they issued a joint statement. In this statement it was declared that South Africa was absolved from any serious misconduct, that there was no oppression or evidence of the native population being exterminated, no signs of militarisation in the territory and that no evidence had been found of any threat to international peace.[173]

On his return to New York Dr. Carpio found himself in very hot water and was forced to retract his joint statement and redraft his report so that South West Africa appeared to be one of the hell holes of Africa. Dr. Carpio claimed that Dr. Verwoerd had lured and pressured him into signing the statement. He also alleged that his coffee had been poisoned in Pretoria. Meanwhile Dr. Carpio's fellow committee member, Dr. de Alva, stood by the original report which he said was accurate, and the whole mission was allowed to degenerate into a farce of comical proportions.[174]

---

[172] *Verwoerd só onthou ons hom, op.cit.*, 130.
[173] F. Barnard, *op.cit.*, 155 and J. Botha, *op.cit.*, 227.
[174] S.E.D. Brown, U.N. Mission That Miscarried The Carpio Comedy – A Victory For South Africa, *The South African Observer*, July 1962, 1-2.

South West Africa Case at The Hague (Part 1)

On 4 November 1960 Ethiopia and Liberia,[175] acting as front men on behalf of the international bankers, brought a case against South Africa in the International Court of Justice in The Hague alleging that the League of Nations mandate still existed, and that South Africa had failed to promote the interests of its inhabitants, and had therefore forfeited its rights to continue its mandate.[176] These arguments were prepared by Professor Vernon Mackay of the Carnegie Endowment for International Peace who also worked for the CIA.

That Ethiopia was one of the plaintiffs bordered on the theatre of the absurd for the following reasons:-

(i) In May 1941 the 1st South African Division of the South African Army led by Major General George Brink [177] was largely responsible for the liberation of Ethiopia from the Italians.
(ii) Ethiopia was one of the most impoverished countries in the world with a literacy rate of less than 7%.[178]
(iii) Public hangings took place regularly, there was a system of rampant slavery and one third of the national budget was stolen by public officials.[179]

In Liberia, the other plaintiff, an oligarchy of 12,000 former American Negroes, lorded it over its hapless inhabitants of 1.2 million.[180] In December 1962 the Court dismissed these objections in a 7-6 vote, a decision which was quite possibly influenced by the Carpio debacle which had taken place earlier in the year.

Odendaal Commission

On 27 January 1964 the Odendaal Commission headed by the Administrator of Transvaal, Frans Hendrik Odendaal, issued its report on the future development of South West Africa. It proposed a five year economic plan at a cost of R152 million and the creation of 12 territorial homelands, one for each ethnic group. The recommendations were adopted by the South African government.[181]

---

175 Ethiopia and Liberia were used as plaintiffs as they had been members of the League of Nations.
176 Although not obligatory South Africa had continued to rule South West Africa in terms of its original mandate.
177 C. Birkby, *Uncle George The Boer Boyhood, Letters and Battles of Lieutenant-General George Edwin Brink*, Jonathan Ball Publishers, Johannesburg, 1987, 99-157.
178 D.H. Shinn & T.P. Ofcansky, *Historical Dictionary of Ethiopia*, Scarecrow Press Inc., Lanham, Maryland, 2013, 302. This was the rate in 1974 and was probably even lower in 1962.
179 S.E.D. Brown, No Longer Any Honesty, Says Waring, *The South African Observer*, November 1962, 14.
180 S.E.D. Brown, 'Die Burger' Lectures Government On U.N. Approach, *The South African Observer*, August, 1963, 3.
181 J. Botha, *op.cit.*, 232-233.

SOUTH WEST AFRICA CASE AT THE HAGUE (PART 2)

On 6 April 1965 the second phase of the case was resumed. In the strategic planning of the case Dr. Verwoerd played a prominent role.[182] South Africa ably defended its position under the leadership of Advocate David de Villiers and his assistants Pik Botha[183] and Riaan Eksteen. A written presentation of 3,000 pages was made and 15 witnesses out of 38 presented were called. The plaintiffs, led by Advocate Ernest Gross, who was also a member of the secretive Council on Foreign Relations (CFR), alleged that the non-Whites of South West Africa were being deliberately oppressed and exploited, but were not prepared to test these claims under cross examination. These allegations were so comprehensively refuted by the defendant's counsel that the plaintiffs had no other alternative, but to withdraw them. Three days before the judgement the American ambassador in Pretoria sent the South African government, an *aide memoire* which stated that it was expected that the different parties would abide by the Court's decision, which the United States said it would be obliged to support. This message was clearly issued on the basis that the decision would be against South Africa and that if South Africa did not comply with it, the infamous war plan[184] of the tax-exempt Carnegie Endowment for International Peace would be implemented.

On 18 July 1966 the Court delivered its judgement. In a 6-6 split decision the president of the Court, Sir Percy Spender of Australia, used his casting vote. He held that Ethiopia and Liberia had not established any interest and had no *locus standi in judicio* for bringing charges that South Africa had violated its mandate. After the judgement the American ambassador, Arthur Goldberg, debased himself by encouraging the African states in the UNO not to submit to the decision.[185] Nonetheless this judgement was a resounding victory for South Africa, which forced the CIA to employ Plan B. Six weeks later the first terrorist attack took place on the northern border of South West Africa.[186]

---

182 *Verwoerd só onthou ons hom*, *op.cit.*, 139.
183 In 1980 the author attended a meeting of the National Party held in the Johannesburg City Hall and asked Pik Botha if he knew about the Council on Foreign Relations, the Bilderbergers and The Trilateral Commission, and if these organisations were exerting any pressure on South Africa. He replied that he knew about these organisations, but said that they had no influence on South Africa's affairs.
184 See S.E.D. Brown, Carnegie Blueprint For War On South Africa, *The South African Observer*, September 1965, 2, 6-7. This 170 page battle manual was published in August 1965 under the title *Apartheid and United Nations Collective Measures*. In the foreward, the president of the Carnegie Endowment for International Peace, Dr. Joseph E. Johnson, said that the blueprint had been drawn up because there was an "explosive situation" in South Africa and "the impact that situation may have on the prospects for peace and on the future of the U.N.". It was estimated that the UNO military force would need 30,000 assault soldiers, 60,000 reservists, 3,000 air assault forces, 60 warships, 300 fighter planes, 45 attack transports, 35 support vessels, etc. According to the *Chicago Tribune* of 24 July 1965 there would first be a six month air and naval blockade costing $165,672,000 followed by a 30 day blitzkrieg to turn over the country to the non-Whites, costing $94,537,000. Casualties were estimated at about 500. In an article in the *The South African Observer* of November 1965 written by P.N. James and titled More Light on Carnegie Blueprint For War on S.A., it was revealed that the US Army had cleared the direct military aspects of the intervention. The commandant of the United States Military Academy at West Point Major S.C. Sarkesian was quoted as saying that the blueprint had been undertaken "in the best interests of scholarly research".
185 J.A. Marais, *op.cit.*, 172.
186 *Ibid.*, 121.

RIVONIA TRIAL

On 13 July 1963 the security police raided the headquarters of *Umkhonto we Sizwe* (Assegaai of the People), the military wing of the African National Congress (ANC) at Lilliesleaf Farm[187] in Rivonia, an outlying suburb of Johannesburg. There they discovered over a hundred maps detailing potential targets for sabotage such as police stations, post offices, Bantu Affairs offices, power stations, electricity pylons and railway and telephone cables.[188] 193 of these proposed acts of sabotage had already taken place. They also found a document titled *Operation Mayibuye,* which was based partly on *The Palmach* (Strike Companies), which were used to undermine the British mandated territory of Palestine. According to this plan of attack 7,000 well armed terrorists would be brought in by air and ship. Two areas in the Cape Province and one each in Natal and Transvaal would serve as bases. The national command was responsible for securing 48,000 anti-personnel mines, 210,000 hand grenades, 1,500 timing devices, 144 tons of ammonium nitrate, 21.6 tons of aluminium powder and one ton of black powder. As the chief prosecutor, Dr. Percy Yutar, said at the subsequent trial, "production requirements" for munitions for a six-month period were sufficient to blow up the whole of Johannesburg.[189]

The following persons were arrested Govan Mbeki, Raymond Mhlaba, Andrew Mlangeni, Elias Motsoaledi (Blacks), Ahmed Kathrada (Indian), Lionel Bernstein, Hilliard Festenstein, Arthur Goldreich, Denis Goldberg, Bob Hepple, James Kantor and Harold Wolpe (Whites). It is noteworthy that all these white revolutionaries were Jews.[190]

---

187 The farm was owned by Arthur Goldreich and is now a museum which has been heavily subsidised by the US government.
188 M. Brokensha and R. Knowles, *The Fourth of July Raids*, Simondium Publishers, Cape Town, 1965. This book provides details of the activities of the *African Resistance Movement* which blew up electricity pylons and railway signal cables in the Western Cape between September 1963 and June 1964.
189 G. Frankel, *Rivonia's Children: Three Families and the Cost of Conscience in White South Africa*, Jacana Media, Johannesburg, 2011, 258 and G. Ludi and B. Grobbelaar, *The Amazing Mr Fischer*, Nasionale Boekhandel, Cape Town, 1966, 40-44. The latter book details the prominent role Fischer played in the leadership of the banned South African Communist Party. After Fischer spent the years 1932-1937 studying under the auspices of a Rhodes scholarship at New College, Oxford, he returned a changed man. He lacked the intelligence to understand that he was nothing more than a dupe of the international bankers.
190 S. Davidson, The Role of the Jews in South Africa since 1948, *The Occidental Quarterly*, Vol. 11, No.2, Summer 2011, 87. "Mandela's entire development was guided by Jewish 'handlers'. From his early legal career to his adoption of terrorist tactics to his eventual imprisonment, Jews provided indispensable support. Even after he was released from prison, the grey eminence of Harry Oppenheimer persuaded him to change his far-left economic viewpoint in favour of privatizations". I.Benson, op.cit., xiii reinforces this statement as follows: "Right from the beginning the Blacks, like Mandela, have had only one role: that of masking the reality of a Jewish nationalist revolutionary war of conquest; exactly the same has been the role of countless soft-headed Western 'liberals' and 'progressives'". On page xiv Benson writes: "Certainly, it requires no great intelligence to see and understand that the South African Communist Party (SACP)with its team of highly trained revolutionary activists, all drawing orchestrated encouragement and support from the centres of high finance in the West, is on the 'attack' side of the conflict, while the ANC is nothing but the mindless human medium in which the 'alien invader' exercises his powerful techniques".

Their participation conforms to a pattern dating back to at least the English Civil War in the 1640s[191] where Jews have consistently played a prominent role in almost all revolutions and wars since that time. It is possible that some of them are motivated by idealism and may genuinely believe that they are advancing a worthwhile cause, but very few of them realise that they are nothing more than the useful idiots or patsies of the international banking fraternity. The ANC is and always has been a Jewish outfit masquerading as a liberation movement, but employed solely for the benefit of the plutocrats.[192] The trial lasted from October 1963 to April 1964. The principal charge was that the accused had recruited persons for training in the preparation and use of explosives and in terrorist warfare for the purposes of violent revolution and committing acts of sabotage. The defence team was lead by Advocate Bram Fischer, a Rhodes scholar, who was responsible for writing Mandela's three hour speech, which the latter read out from the dock on 20 April 1964.

Those found guilty of sabotage, including Nelson Mandela, the premier puppet of the international bankers, who was already serving a five year term of imprisonment, were sentenced to long terms of imprisonment or life. Goldreich, the leader and mastermind of the conspiracy to overthrow the South African Government, and Wolpe escaped before the trial took place. Unaccountably, the prosecution laid charges of the lesser offence of sabotage against the defendants, and not treason. If the latter charges had been laid, Mandela and his co-defendants would have received, in terms of the then existing law, the death penalty.

On 16 June 1964 Dr. Verwoerd commented on presiding judge Dr. Quartus de Wet's judgement in parliament as follows: "These people are criminals, Communist criminals…When it is said in these circles that they are glad that Mandela received a life-long sentence and not the death penalty, because he may later, like Kenyatta, become a leader of the future, then I say, God forbid it".[193]

---

191 S.M. Goodson, *A History of Central Banking and the Enslavement of Mankind,* Black House Publishing Ltd, London, 2014, 29-41.

192 "In retrospect, the group behavior of Jews in apartheid South Africa conforms very closely to patterns that emerged during the United States Civil Rights Movement and continue to emerge in Europe's current drive towards a non-White multicultural entity. Understanding Jewish influence on the decline of the West and responding to it effectively will likely prove decisive factors whether Whites once again establish the integrity of their nations — or continue to be outmanoeuvred and ultimately dispossessed", *The Occidental Quarterly, op.cit.,* 88. In December 1960 in a large vacant house near Zoo Lake, Johannesburg, the South African Communist Party held its annual congress. At this meeting the Jewish leadership announced that the armed struggle would commence. Sitting at the back of the room were Nelson Mandela and Walter Sisulu, who were shocked to hear this decision, as the policy of the ANC as articulated by its leader Albert Luthuli, was that the movement was against any form of violence, 1960 An excerpt from Thula Simpson's newly published book, Umkhonto we Sizwe: The ANC's Armed Struggle, *Noseweek,* April 2016. See also G.Ludi and B. Grobbelaar, *op.cit.,* 88 where *A Draft Discussion Document* found in the possession of Bram Fischer states that one of the immediate tasks of the SACP [in 1965] "is to help rebuild fronts, especially the ANC" and S. Goodson, The ANC a Liberation Movement or A Tool of the Bankers, *Impact Magazine,* April/May 2013, 1-2.

193 J.A. Marais, *op.cit.,* 122.

SCANDINAVIAN FOREIGN MINISTERS

In early September 1963 Dr. Verwoerd sent confidential invitations to the foreign ministers of Denmark, Finland, Iceland, Norway and Sweden to visit South Africa at the latter's expense. They would be free to see what they liked and speak to whomsoever they wished because "South Africa has nothing of which to be ashamed of or to hide away.[194]

However, instead of replying directly to the South African government, these Scandinavian countries in an act of dismaying discourtesy, issued a joint press statement in which they refused to send any representatives. They said that they wanted "to continue judging South Africa's policy without firsthand knowledge". Dr. Verwoerd replied that he could not imagine "a weaker or more wrong excuse than that which they had given. It is clear that the real reason for their refusal is that they are afraid of the truth, and to testify to it. They are afraid to base their judgment impartially on the real facts of South African policy. We set the test – they failed to pass it".[195] Dr. Verwoerd concluded that "The whole world now knows that they are a people who pretend to be impartial and honest, but who prefer to stay away so that they can say what they like and only make as if they know. But in the end truth must and will triumph in spite of disappointments".[196]

SIMON'S TOWN NAVAL AGREEMENT

Dr. Verwoerd believed that a strong foreign policy determined the maintenance of stable internal policies.[197] On 15 March 1963 Harold Wilson, who was at that time leader of the opposition Labour Party, announced in a speech at Trafalgar Square, London that if his party came to power, all arms exports to South Africa would be forbidden.

---

194 J. Botha, *op cit.*, 110.
195 S.E.D. Brown, Nordic Countries 'Afraid To See The Truth about S.A.', says Verwoerd, *The South African Observer*, October 1963, 16.
196 J. Botha, *op.cit.*, 110. Ironically, Sweden, which has an ever-increasing non-White population of at least 17%, faces a self-inflicted and insoluble racial problem. http://dailycaller.com/2014/11/02/swedish-police-release-extensive-report-detailing-control-of-55-no-go-zones-by-muslim-criminal-gangs/
197 Cf. *"Ezra Pound Speaking"*, Radio Speeches of World War II, edited by L.W. Doob, Greenwood Press, Connecticut, Westport, Connecticut, 1978, 403 in which Pound quotes Vidkun Quisling's famous axiom: "The influence of a state in foreign politics always corresponds to the degree of development of its INTERNAL strength".

On 15 October 1964 the Labour Party defeated the Conservative Party in a general election. Mr. Wilson reiterated his undertaking not to supply South Africa with arms, and in particular the export of 16 Buccaneer[198] S.50s long range low level attack aircraft, which had been purchased under the Simon's Town Naval Agreement. Previously in a speech he gave at Pietersburg on 2 July 1964 Dr. Verwoerd warned Mr. Wilson that if the aircraft were not delivered, he would terminate the Simon's Town Naval Agreement.

After consulting his naval chiefs, Mr. Wilson backed down and allowed the export of the aircraft to proceed. An option to purchase a further 16 Buccaneers was not allowed and as a result thereof redundancies had to be instituted at the Hawker Siddeley factory in Brough, England.

In 1964 Harold Wilson, Prime Minister of Great Britain, threatened to renege on a contract to supply the South African Air Force with 16 Buccaneer S.2 maritime strike aircraft. When Dr. Verwoerd indicated that he would cancel the Simon's Town Agreement, which allowed Royal Navy vessels to use the naval base, Wilson quickly climbed down.

FREEMASONRY

In July 1964 Dr. Verwoerd agreed, at the suggestion of the Leader of the Opposition, Sir de Villiers Graaff, to appoint a judicial commission to investigate the influence and activities of all secret organisations, which included the Freemasons, the Broederbond and the Sons of England, and to determine if these bodies were a danger to the state or peace.

Dr. Verwoerd formulated the guidelines which the commission had to follow and in its report submitted to parliament, it was found that freemasonry "was not a danger to the state nor to the peace of the nation".[199]

---

198 Dr. Verwoerd named his motor boat kept at his farm on the banks of the Vaal river, *Boekanier*. A. Boshoff, *Sekretaresse Vir Die Verwoerds,* Human & Rousseau, Kaapstad, 1974, 192.
199 A.A. Cooper, *The Freemasons of South Africa,* Human & Rousseau, Cape Town, 1986, 180. See also *Verwoerd só onthou ons hom*, op.cit., F. Coetzer, Dr. Verwoerd en Binnelandse Veiligheid, 148-149.

In April 1965 the US Navy requested that the *USS Independence*, an aircraft carrier of 60,000 tons, be allowed to take on bunker oil at Cape Town docks. They also asked that their Negro sailors be allowed to disembark. Dr. Verwoerd considered this request to be a provocation and the carrier was denied permission to dock.

USS INDEPENDENCE

In April 1965 the US government tried to embarrass Dr. Verwoerd when it requested that the aircraft carrier *USS Independence* be allowed to take on bunker fuel at Cape Town harbour. It also requested that Negro sailors be permitted to take shore leave and that Negro members of the air crews be allowed to land on local airfields. Dr. Verwoerd refused to accede to this unmistakable provocation. The ship was refused entry and had to refuel in mid-ocean at great expense to the United States Navy.[200] Dr. Verwoerd would not tolerate any American interference in the internal affairs of South Africa and in March 1966 he expelled two American diplomats, O'Shiel and Witt, who were undercover CIA operatives, who had been inciting black people to commit violence in South West Africa.[201] There was nothing unusual in Dr. Verwoerd applying this policy. In 1951 when the United States Navy set up a naval air station in Keflevik, Iceland, the Icelandic government insisted that no Negroes be stationed on the island,[202] while up to the late 1990s black crew members of tankers were refused permission to disembark. The Icelanders wished to retain the homogeneity of their Celtic/Nordic forebears and to protect their gene pool.

200 J. Botha, *op.cit.*, 125.
201 P.C. Swanepoel, *op.cit.*, 112-113.
202 The US Air Force requested that no Negroes of any branch be sent to Iceland, Greenland or Labrador. Office of the Chief of Military History, US Army, 1966.

Sport Policy

The policy of separate development in sport, which was in concurrence with traditional practice, was organised on a racial basis. In his New Year's speech in 1964 Dr. Verwoerd warned that "The purpose of those who attack our policy of separation is clear; it is to use sport as a means of forcing racial integration on us. We must not allow our attackers to frighten us, for we are involved in a life and death struggle".

In June – September 1965 while a Springbok rugby team was touring New Zealand, the possibility was raised in the media that Maoris could form part of the New Zealand team on their next tour to South Africa in 1967. In a speech[203] given at Loskop Dam in the Eastern Transvaal on 4 September 1965, Dr. Verwoerd stated unambiguously that when South African teams toured overseas as guests, and when it was the custom to include non-Whites, such as Maoris, in the host's team that was entirely acceptable. When teams visited South Africa, they were expected to abide by South African norms and traditions and not include non-Whites.

As we may observe once again, Dr. Verwoerd refused to yield on principle and was frequently described or depicted in cartoons as a man of granite.[204] He would often hold up the example of the Federation of Rhodesia and Nyasaland,[205] which initially made a number of small concessions and eventually crumbled. On the other hand Dr. Verwoerd could be flexible when, for example, he overruled the caucus who wished to maintain a prohibition on the sale of alcohol to black people. He said that prohibition was creating enmity against the police and bedevilling race relations and that the ban therefore had to be lifted. It is quite possible that the nine policemen who were murdered in a raid for illicit liquor at Cato Manor, Durban in January 1960 prompted this change in policy.

Rhodesia's Unilateral Declaration of Independence

On 11 November 1965 Rhodesia unilaterally declared her independence. Prior to the declaration Dr. Verwoerd refrained from any comments about the dispute. In a speech he gave to parliament on 25 January 1966, Dr. Verwoerd said that South Africa would continue to maintain good neighbourly relations with

---

203 Toespraak deur Dr H. F. Verwoerd by die Nasionale Jeugbondkongres te Loskopdam, 4 September 1965, 18-19.
204 J. Botha, *op.cit.*, Chap. Two, Hendrik Verwoerd, Man of Granite, 10-44.
205 S.E.D. Brown, "Necessary To Prepare S.A.'s Defences", says Verwoerd, *The South African Observer*, April 1962, 8.

Rhodesia and South Africa's policy of non-intervention in the internal affairs of other nations. Moreover, South Africa would not participate in any sanctions or boycotts and would continue to trade with both Britain and Rhodesia.

Dr. Verwoerd rejected the notion that South Africa should act as a mediator, as inevitably the one party would be preferred to the other. He noted that there was no similarity between the policy of separate development and the Rhodesian policy of partnership, and warned that the latter would lead to "tragedy".[206] He also made the following prediction: "I say unequivocally that we believe that majority rule there, which means a Black government ruling over the Whites, will lead to destruction and chaos".[207]

Since 2000 when over 3,000 white owned farms were seized without payment of any compensation, the size of the economy of Rhodesia, now known as Zimbabwe, has halved.[208] During the mid-1970s one Rhodesian dollar was worth one British pound, but after hyperinflation reached a world record high of 231 million percent in 2008, the currency became worthless and has been abandoned and replaced by foreign currencies.

Poverty is at desperate levels. Over half the population of 13 million is severely undernourished and 90% of the work force is without gainful employment.[209] Most civil and human rights have been abrogated.

UNITED STATES SOUTH AFRICA LEADERS EXCHANGE PROGRAM

Ever since the Nationalists assumed power in 1948 the United States had adopted a long term strategy to undermine the White government and replace it with a regime of black puppets. In January 1958 the Council on Foreign Relations set up the United States South Africa Leader Exchange Program (USSALEP). It was run from the offices of the notorious *African American Institute* which as we have already seen was responsible for the Sharpeville riot. The programme was an exchange scheme for leaders of the United States and South Africa and was later expanded to include, mainly journalists, and in total 53 South African journalists would be sent to the United States as Nieman fellows. These journalists were trained to brainwash the Afrikaner people in the tenets of liberalism and ultimately to condition them to accept the dictates of the New World Order.

---

206 J.A. Marais, *op.cit.*, 92. A. Sparks, *The Mind of South Africa The Story of the Rise and Fall of Apartheid*, William Heinemann Ltd, London, 1990, 50, 249. In these extracts, Sparks, a prominent liberal and former editor of the defunct *Rand Daily Mail*, holds up an independent Zimbabwe as a success story, which can be emulated in South Africa as well, but he has turned out to be wrong in both instances.
207 J.A. Marais, *op.cit.*, 91.
208 *Business Reporter*, 29 October 2015, p. 20.
209 http://www.indexmundi.com/zimbabwe/unemployment_rate.html

Dr. Verwoerd and Ian Smith at Libertas, Pretoria on 2 July 1964, shortly after the latter had been elected prime minister of Southern Rhodesia. Dr. Verwoerd warned that majority rule would be a disaster, but Smith stubbornly persisted with his *sub rosa* plan to achieve that outcome.

Some of the key figures serving on the South African committee of this sinister organisation were Mr. D.P. De Villiers[210], managing director of Nasionale Pers, Dr. Anton Rupert, chairman of the Rembrandt Tobacco Corporation, Dr. F.E.W Schumann, vice chairman S.A. Atomic Energy Board, Professor H.B. Thom, principal of the University of Stellenbosch, Dr. H.J. van Eck, chairman Industrial Development Corporation and Dr. A.D. Wassenaar, general manager Sanlam.

A sister organisation of the USSALEP was the American Field Service. Founded in 1948 in its present format and endorsed by the United States State Department, its avowed purpose has always been "to promote world peace through international understanding".[211] However, its real aim has always been to identify young boys and girls in their matriculation year at school, who have leadership potential, and to inculcate them with liberal ideas.[212]

In August 1966, shortly before Dr. Verwoerd's assassination, fellow MP, Jaap Marais, asked Dr. Verwoerd what should be done about USSALEP. He replied: *"Dit moet gebreek word. Ek wag net my tyd daarvoor af"*. (It must be broken. I am just waiting for my opportunity).[213] Unfortunately Dr. Verwoerd did not live to enable the crushing out of existence of this subversive organisation which continued to operate until 2003.

<u>CULTURE</u>

Dr. Verwoerd had a profound interest in the preservation, maintenance and development of all forms of culture. On 8 April 1959 he officiated[214] at The Castle, South Africa's oldest building, in the establishment of the Simon van der Stel Foundation. The most important task of this foundation was to raise funds to purchase, conserve and where necessary restore buildings of historic and aesthetic interest. He said that the foundation should also encourage the formation of organisations to protect the historical buildings and artefacts of other races and mentioned in particular, the Malay Quarter in Cape Town and the Emakuzeni in the valley of the Zulu kings who are buried there.

---

210 I. Benson, Gary Allen, Gary Allen!, *Behind The News*, March 1978, 1-2 and S.E.D. Brown, U.S. Leader Exchange Programme – And Double Talk, *The South African Observer*, November 1965, 2. In 1974 P.W. Botha, who was Minister of Defence at that time, referred in a speech to some of the subversive activities of the CFR mentioned in Dan Smoot's *Invisible Government*, which the writer, a former FBI agent, self-published in 1962. Mr. Botha was castigated in a most ferocious manner by the English language press as well as some Afrikaans newspapers. He was then spoken to by Advocate D. P. de Villiers and warned never to raise this subject again, with the implied threat that if he did so, he would jeopardize his political career. Extract from a speech given by Ivor Benson at The Southern Africa Solidarity Conference held in Pretoria on 29-30 November 1974.
211 C. Nissen (Pseudonym of Ivor Benson,) Leftist 'Orientation' Course For South African Scholars, *The South African Observer*, August 1963, 5.
212 In 1965 the author was shortlisted for a scholarship. Fortunately his date of birth fell out of the required age group by seven days and he did not participate.
213 J.A. Marais, *op.cit.*, 144.
214 *Verwoerd aan die Woord*, *op.cit.*, 249-253.

Dr. Verwoerd was a connoisseur of classical music, ballet and opera and attended performances regularly.[215]

Television

In a speech[216] given in parliament on 9 March 1960, Dr. Verwoerd explained the government's position on the introduction of television. He said that it was a non-essential service and that it would be advantageous to let other countries bear the experimental and developmental costs, including the transition from black and white to colour. He also mentioned the obstacles in providing a service for the whole country and a fair service for each language group and that television would have an adverse effect on attendance at certain sporting events. He said that commercial television would lead to a lowering of cultural standards, particularly if programmes were imported from the United States. He also emphasised the dangers of a "yellow" TV developing, similar to the yellow press. He cited an American survey which found that television advertising had raised the cost of living and the cost of some goods by 25%.

On 14 August 1963 Mrs. Margaret Baird, widow of John Logie Baird the inventor of television, defended the South African Government's attitude to television at a London press conference. The following month when she visited South Africa for a five month visit, she praised the South African Broadcasting Corporation, which she found to be "dignified and not impersonal". She also said that some of the programmes on British television "are too sordid for words" and when asked if South Africa should have television, she replied: "In a lovely country like that, why should we sit inside and watch cowboys on television?"[217]

Dr. Verwoerd said that patience was necessary. Another 16 years would pass before television was inaugurated in 1976. He foresaw that old films would be continually recycled. Although he lived before the advent of the internet, it is a fact that this medium of communication has displaced television to an ever-increasing extent; hastened in no small measure by the poor quality of many programmes and the unremitting bias in news reporting world-wide.[218]

---

215 During May 1966 Dr. Verwoerd attended the following performances in Pretoria: *Nabucco, Die Fledermaus, Cinderella* and *Die Pluimsaad Waai Ver.* A. Boshoff, op.cit., 212. According to world renowned soprano opera singer, Mimi Coertse, who was a lifelong friend of Dr. Verwoerd, "he appreciated good music." *Verwoerd só onthou ons hom, op.cit.*, M. Coertse, Op 'N Persoonlike Noot, 216.
216 *Verwoerd aan die Woord, op.cit.*, 321-346.
217 S.E.D. Brown, TV Not Essential In S.A., says Mrs Baird , *The South African Observer*, 8 September 1963.
218 http://www.businessinsider.com/wait-did-cnn-just-lose-half-of-its-viewers-2012-3 8 David Seaman, the writer of this article writes as follows: "...this is what happens to you when you continue to report stories that no longer resemble - even remotely - what your own viewers see outside their windows and apartments". See also How the Media Shaped the Generations: Radio & the Teenager (2017) https://www.youtube.com/watch?v=blYD_o9uQn8

Economics

Dr. Verwoerd was familiar with South Africa's economic problems and was conscious of the fact that racial peace was dependent on prosperity being enjoyed by all its inhabitants. Rapid industrialisation was one of the key components in order to realise this objective and to attain greater economic sovereignty. He was also aware of South Africa's dependency on exports of raw materials and agricultural products, and realised that the solution, in this instance, lay in the beneficiation of minerals and the expansion of import replacement industries. Long term planning and the improved use of capital formed an integral part of Dr. Verwoerd's thinking. He set up an economics section[219] in the prime minister's department which worked closely with the Economic Council of Advisers.

During his premiership the infrastructure was considerably enhanced with the planning and building of new Eskom power stations (R160 million),[220] a third Iscor steel plant (R540 million), a second Sasol oil from coal plant (R60 million), expansion of the telephone network (R100 million), the founding of Foskor (phosphate mining and chemical production), the establishment of the Atlas Aircraft Corporation and the Orange River Scheme (R450 million), which resulted in the construction of the largest dam in South Africa with a storage capacity of 5,230,000 mega litres. In 1971 the dam was named the H F Verwoerd Dam. On 16 May 1962 Dr. Verwoerd spoke[221] in English at the Convention for the Promotion of Export Trade held at the Wanderers Club in Johannesburg. He addressed an audience of 500 prominent businessmen and economists who were mainly English-speaking. As usual he spoke without the assistance of notes and revealed a detailed and thorough knowledge of the export trade and how it should be advanced for the benefit of everyone. At the end of his speech Dr. Verwoerd received a standing ovation which lasted three minutes.

Environment

Dr. Verwoerd was a devout conservationist and innate lover of nature. When the Transvaal Roads Department wanted to remove a giant harpephyllum tree which lay in the path of the proposed national road near Zoutpansberg, he instructed the department to build the road around the tree. When some shady businessmen tried to privatise the western half of the Kruger National Park for cattle ranching, he intervened immediately and forbade any changes to the boundaries of the park.

---

219 *Verwoerd aan die Woord, op.cit.*, 585. He also had his own scientific adviser.
220 £1=R2
221 *Verwoerd aan die Woord, op.cit.*, 648-663.

In 1954 a Marine Reserve was established not far from Dr. Verwoerd's holiday home, Blaas ń Bietjie (Rest a Little,) in Betty's Bay, Western Cape. The reserve was later named after him.

Dr. Verwoerd's favourite recreation was angling. Here he is seen outside his seaside cottage, Blaas-'n-Bietjie, on his way to catch fish from the rocks at Betty's Bay. (His fishing rods are still stored at the back of the garage).

Chapter VI

THE INTERNATIONAL MONEY POWER
SOUTH AFRICA FOUNDATION

In July 1951 Harry Oppenheimer established the United South Africa Trust Fund. It raised £1 million (R2 million) and its initial purpose was to defeat the National Party in the 1953 election. After that venture failed, the trust focused its attention on more general democratic ideals such as fostering understanding between the different races, convincing all South Africans of their interdependence and common interests, undertaking research into the racial, social and economic problems of South Africa and provision of financial support for the opposition United Party or any other political party which strove for racial co-operation.

In 1960 Harry Oppenheimer realised that attempts to defeat the National Party at the polls were pointless and he therefore adopted a different approach by setting up the South Africa Foundation[222] in place of the United Trust Fund. It was established by Oppenheimer with ten of his business friends and later leading Afrikaners in business and academia, such as W.B. Coetzer (General Mining), M.S. Louw (Santam), Jan S. Marais (Trust Bank), Anton Rupert[223] (Rembrandt Tobacco), H.B. Thom (University of Stellenbosch) and H.J. van Eck (Industrial Development Corporation) were recruited.

In an article titled Portrait of a Millionaire: I, Harry Oppenheimer in the April-June 1960 issue of *Africa South*[224] (Vol. 4 no. 3) and written in the first person, Harry Oppenheimer, who was once described by the editor of *The South African Observer*, S.E.D. Brown, as "the deadliest enemy of our national survival",[225] laid out his plans to destroy Dr. Verwoerd and the government's policy of separate development. He wrote *inter alia*:

> "Once the air has been cleared of animosities, we will be able, too, to pave the way for a merger of the two sections. This is, after all, the only safe way to get rid of Dr. Verwoerd . All other methods will merely consolidate his

---

222 S.E.D. Brown, An Open letter To Sir Francis De Guigand, *The South African Observer*, April 1966, 1-3. In his open letter to Sir Francis, S.E.D. Brown described the foundation as a "plush liberal club where prominent people from both language groups can come together".
223 In 1970 the author had a short term assignment at Rupert International and once observed Anton Rupert working at his papers in the board room. He had a weak handshake and was apparently dominated by his wife Huberte. He was well known for his parsimoniousness.
224 P.C. Swanepoel, *op.cit.*, 240-243. The writer states that *Africa South* was financed by the Congress for Cultural Freedom, which was in turn financed by the CIA. The magazine founded and edited by Ronald Segal was published by Africa South Publications (Pty) Ltd in Cape Town. The first issue appeared in Oct.-Dec. 1956. In June 1960 it was banned and reappeared in London as *Africa South in Exile*. See also A. Parker, CIA-backed Ronald Segal top propagandist, *The Citizen*, Johannesburg, 1977, 50-52.
225 S.E.D. Brown, No Comfort For Forces Of Conservatism, *The South African Observer*, August 1966, 3.

position; we must undermine him from within. To sum up: the immediate task of the South Africa Foundation is to create an atmosphere in which it will be possible to arrange a coalition of the moderate elements in the Government and the Opposition.[226]

"In effect, the advent of the South Africa Foundation reflects the return of big business to active politics. It is high time. My business colleagues have let the situation deteriorate for far too long."[227]

"Verwoerd, admittedly, can be ousted with the help of the non-whites, but that means sharing the victory with them. Are any liberals prepared to pay that price? And it will be a heavy price! Trying to remove Verwoerd through the ballot box is utterly futile: this is accepted, I think by all shades of opinion. Is there any real alternative, therefore, to the 'merger of moderates' which the Foundation proposes?[228]

"Picture the industrial revolution that will take place in Africa if the black man's economic fetters are struck from! Think of the millions of skilled men who will enter the labour market. Think of the vast new consuming public!"[229] "I think that I can claim the main credit for this exciting vision of the new Africa; yet all that I have done, really, is to allow myself to be guided by the interests of Anglo American. Are you still unconvinced? How can what is good for Anglo American[230] possibly be bad for South Africa?"[231]

Why did Harry Oppenheimer want to eliminate Dr. Verwoerd? In January 1957 while still a United Party member of parliament, he gave a speech at Oxford University, which indicated that his thinking was little different from that of the National Party when he said that: "Our growing industrial needs must make full use of Bantu labour, and we must not worry overmuch about the consequences, because the Native is, on the whole so uncivilized that the white man will remain on top for as long as we can see at the moment".[232] In 1960 he had stated in a leading American journal *US News and World Report*

---

226 H. F. Oppenheimer, *op.cit.*, 14.
227 *Ibid.*, 14.
228 *Ibid.*, 16.
229 *Ibid.*, 16.
230 Fifty years later Anglo American is only a shadow of its former self. A decade ago, at the peak of the commodities boom, Anglo American paid top dollar prices for investments in coal, copper and iron ore mines. Since then the bottom has fallen out of the markets for these base metals, as well as platinum. In order to stave off imminent bankruptcy, the corporation has been forced to sell 30 of its 55 mining assets and reduce its work force from 135,000 to 50,000 persons. Meanwhile its share price in London has fallen by 92.5% from a peak of £36.83 on 19 May 2008 to £2.78 on 9 December 2015. The former mining house "giant" is so broke that it can no longer afford to print hard copies of its in-house quarterly magazine *Optima*, which has been published since 1951. On 17 February 2016 Fitch Ratings downgraded Anglo American's credit rating to "junk" status.
231 H.F. Oppenheimer, *op.cit.*, 16.
232 S.E.D. Brown, New U.P. Leadership – But Nothing New, *The South African Observer*, February 1957, 5.

that he recognised the merits of Dr. Verwoerd's policies, when he said that "What the South African government was trying to do in separating the black and white races was not necessarily immoral as partition had provided the answer to problems in many parts of the world".[233]

Furthermore in a speech he gave at Kitwe on the Copperbelt in Northern Rhodesia in 1961, Mr. Oppenheimer said that "What the Congo does show is that primitive, uncivilised people cannot be trusted with the running of a modern state, and that independent democracy is the only possibility if the electorate has reasonable standards of education and civilisation".[234]

In an article in the April 1961 edition of the *The South African Observer*, Ivor Benson exposed Harry Oppenheimer as being a pseudo-liberal and a hypocrite, who could not care less about advancing the welfare of Black people. He wrote that his whole *raison d'etre* was centred on serving the "aims and ends of American Big Money" [235] and the New World Order.

DR. VERWOERD CONFRONTS THE MONEY POWER

A few days after he had been elected Prime Minister on 2 September 1958, Dr. Verwoerd stated in an interview that "one of the most important principles of South Africa's economic policy is to encourage domestic capital formation".[236] In a speech given to the Afrikaanse Handelsinstituut on 19 September 1961 in Pretoria, Dr. Verwoerd warned about the vagaries of foreign investment saying that "Our eyes are not blind to the fact that foreign capital is in a certain sense unknown and not an unmixed blessing. It has the character of a fair weather friend. We have experienced how a portion of that investment capital acts as flight capital when difficulties arise. For that we have no great inclination".[237]

On 17 October 1961 Dr. Verwoerd made a full frontal attack on Harry Oppenheimer, the chairman of the Anglo American Corporation, in the House of Assembly.

"The directors, when they meet, hold private discussions. In the case of such a powerful body there is also a central body which lays down basic policy. The influence of that central body, to say the least, must be great in our economic

---

233 A. Hocking, *Oppenheimer & Son*, McGraw-Hill, Johannesburg, 1973, 353.
234 D. Pallister, S. Stewart, I. Lepper, *South Africa, Inc.: The Oppenheimer Empire*, Yale University Press, New Haven, Connecticut, 1988, 64. In 1987 the book was advertised on South African radio. The Oppenheimers complained and the advertisement was immediately withdrawn.
235 C. Nissen (Pseudonym of Ivor Benson), Oppenheimer's Rôle in S.A,'s Politics, *The South African Observer*, April 1961, 6.
236 J.A. Marais, *op.cit.*, 12.
237 *Verwoerd aan die Woord, op.cit.*, 576.

life. Nobody knows, however, what they discuss there. In the course of his speeches Mr. Oppenheimer, the leader, makes political statements; he discusses political policy, he tries to exercise political influence. He even supports a political party…in other words he has political aims; he wants to steer things in a political direction…He can secretly cause a good many things to happen. In other words, he can pull strings. With all that monetary power and with this powerful machine which is spread over the whole country he can if he so chooses, exercise an enormous influence against the Government and against the State".[238]

Three years later Dr. Verwoerd was able to announce that "The stage has been reached where the normal development of South Africa can be developed with the own savings of the nation".[239] Dr. Verwoerd had achieved the seemingly impossible feat of autarky - sovereign independence and freedom from the parasitic international bankers and their usurious loans.

In August 1963 Harry Oppenheimer allowed the second largest mining house, General Mining and Finance Corporation Ltd to be partially absorbed by Federale Mynbou Bpk, in a merger, valued at R20 million (£10 million), which looked more like a reverse takeover of Federale Mynbou by General Mining.[240] The Johannesburg *Sunday Times* described the takeover as a personal triumph for Mr. Oppenheimer,[241] while Afrikaans newspapers reported it as being "a breakthrough for Afrikaans mining interests".[242] Dr. Verwoerd had a more sober reaction and said that the managing director of Federale Mynbou, Tom Muller, was like a fly on a railway track waiting for a thundering train.[243] It is also relevant to recall what Dr. Verwoerd's predecessor, Advocate J.G. Strydom, once said: "It will be a sad day for South Africa if Afrikaans financiers ever find common ground with Harry Oppenheimer".[244]

On 25 September 1965 at a meeting in his constituency of Heidelberg, Dr. Verwoerd pointed out that South Africa not only had to deal with the International Money Power,[245] but a new money power which was developing in South Africa. He said that it was important that this domestic money power took into account the political conduct and norms of the country, and that it did not drift away from the national interest and become a money power operating exclusively for its own interests. Furthermore he said that "There is a real

---

238 D. Pallister, S. Stewart, I. Lepper, *op.cit.*, 64 .
239 J.A. Marais, *op.cit.*, 12-13. Foreign loans outstanding in 1960 amounted to R2.4 billion compared to R734.1 billion in December 2016.
240 *Ibid.*, 144-145.
241 P.J. Pretorius, *op.cit.*, 153. B.J. Vorster attended the reception celebrating the transaction.
242 *Ibid.*, 145.
243 *Ibid.*, 145.
244 S.E.D. Brown, Our Readers Say, *The South African Observer*, October 1963, 16.
245 J.A. Marais, op.cit., 173. Dr. Verwoerd was not the first leader to condemn the International Money Power. Both President Paul Kruger and Prime Minister JBM Hertzog called the International Money Power an enemy of the people.

S.E.D Brown, was one of South Africa's foremost political thinkers. He was editor of the monthly journal, *The South African Observer* (1955-1992), and relentlessly exposed the treasonous activities of the National Party government after the demise of Dr. Verwoerd.

danger that the South African Money Power will merge with the International Money Power which is alien to South Africa and its people. The country must see to it that the developing Money Power remains faithful to the nation and that it does not clash with the ideals and security of its people". [246]

In one of his last speeches Dr. Verwoerd indicated that he intended to reorganise the financial sector so that it operated in South Africa's interests when he said: "It may be necessary to investigate the structure of banking in South Africa. This will affect banks and insurance companies which have their head offices overseas…Businesses ought to operate in the interest of the country in which they are established".[247]

---

246 P.J. Pretorius, *op.cit.*, 154.
247 *Die Transvaler*, 14 March 1966.

Hoek Report

In 1964 Professor Piet Hoek, a former professor of economics at the University of Pretoria who was working for ISCOR as deputy general manager,[248] warned Dr. Verwoerd that the Rothschild/Oppenheimer controlled Anglo American Corporation was doing everything possible to sabotage his policy of separate development and recommended that a commission of enquiry be appointed. Dr. Verwoerd said that he would prefer to be less confrontational and asked him to write a report and give it to him. This became known as the infamous *Hoek Report*.

The title of the *Hoek Report* reads as follows: *Die Oormatige Konsentrasie van Kapitaal, Produksie, en Mark binne die Invloedsfeer van 'n Enkelbeheergroep, sy Mag om te kan bepaal waar 'n Groot Gedeelte van die Beskikbare Kapitaalsfondse van die Privaatsektor belê sal word en dus waar Werkverskaffing sal wees en nie sal wees nie, en Moontlike Teenmaatreëls* (The Excessive Concentration of Capital, Production, and Market within the Sphere of Influence of a Single Controlling Group, its Power to determine where a Large Portion of the Available Capital Funds of the Private Sector shall be invested and where the Provision of Work shall be, and Possible Counter Measures).

The first 36 pages of this 176 page document contain the main text and the remaining 139 pages contain six annexures. Professor Hoek established the parameters of his thesis in the following paragraphs.

"The demand for labour is a necessity where there is work, and as far as industries, construction and services are concerned, the provision of work is mainly where capital is invested.

"Through a method of functioning which makes it practically impossible to observe it in public and which cannot be exposed without a comprehensive and co-ordinated investigation, a large capital – and concentration of a powerful group of activities, namely the AAC group, as will be shown, has obtained a position in our country where it has gathered under its sphere of influence more than 900[249] companies which include some of the largest in the country. For practical purposes this group has acquired control over the mobilisation of probably the largest portion of the private sector's capital and as a result thereof has obtained the power to decide where that capital shall be invested, with the consequent influence on the influx to and concentration of Non-Whites in specific areas. Where industries and construction play such a large role in

---
[248] P.J. Pretorius, *op.cit.*, 155.
[249] The total number of companies under Anglo American's control was 918.

our provision of additional work and investment capital (in contrast with the mining industry), it was only realistic in the functioning of the AAC-group and as a result of their annual free funds, that this group has in the last few years entered on a large scale the areas where large scale investment is required, namely industry, construction and services, and where as shown caused an influx of labour to where the specific new investment or expansion has taken place.

"If this group [controlling 70% of commerce, industry and mining] which possesses this position of power, as will be shown, should support and purposefully advance the Government's policy which concerns our heterogeneous population and separate development thereof for the peaceful, safe and healthy development of all population groups, then decentralisation of industry and consequently also construction and the complementary services and establishment thereof near the homelands, this would be an obvious success with the consequent large scale provision of work in centres other than the present White cities which are becoming more and more black. The opposite has nevertheless been clearly stated, they will not support the Government's policy[250] as it appears from Mr. Oppenheimer's statement in his Chairman's Report of 1964, namely 'Discrimination on grounds of race or colour is morally wrong and partition on grounds of race or colour is economically impossible'.

"Not only the well known political opinions of the controllers of AAC in Southern Africa, but also the international financial interests in its share capital, which undoubtedly have a controlling influence in AAC, will have no loyalty to the interests of the separate peoples in Southern Africa; on the contrary this holds further dangers, particularly if the historic actions of international banks and international capital are used in connection with the revolutions and riots, for example the organising and financing of the Russian Revolution in 1917, and where they are used in connection with the obsession of international capital with the eradication of national boundaries and differences. In brief, the philosophy of the international capitalist is that nations must work for international capitalism – the philosophy of the nationalist is that capital must work for the nation".[251]

Professor Hoek reported that Anglo American retained most of the dividends it received from its subsidiaries and paid hardly any tax.[252] He also noted that they used unrest, such as the CIA instigated riot at Sharpeville in March 1960, of which Anglo American with its foreign intelligence links quite possibly had

---

250 J.A. Marais, *op.cit.*, 176-179.
251 *Hoek Verslag van Prof. Piet Hoek aan Dr. H.F. Verwoerd, 1965*, 3-4.
252 *Ibid.*, 13.

foreknowledge, to buy shares listed on the stock exchange cheaply.[253] These shares were bought at the expense of the public and AAC's capital gains were not subject to tax.[254] By retaining most of its dividends Anglo American had built up large cash balances. Companies, which could not afford the high interest rates payable on bank loans, were often obliged to approach Anglo American with its cash hoard[255] and ended up being absorbed into its web of subsidiaries. These cash balances were also lent to subsidiaries by means of loan accounts. Anglo American was thus acting as a clearing house and may have been contravening the Banks Act.[256]

(i) Between 1956 and 1965 the percentage of company tax Anglo American paid on its profits amounted to 5.4%,[257] whereas the rate of company taxation at that time was 40%.[258] Anglo American benefited from the fact that profits on the sale of shares were non-taxable,[259] whereas profits of the same nature made by individuals were taxable.[260]

(ii) Anglo American only invested in existing enterprises and not near the homelands, thus deliberately flouting the government's policy of establishing new industries on the borders of the homelands.[261] Professor Hoek realised that Anglo American would continue to resist this policy and that the solution was not to take on individual companies, but the whole group.[262]

He proposed the following measures which he believed would drastically reduce the power and influence of Anglo American.

(i) All dividends to be taxed at company rates of taxation.[263]
(ii) Increases in the market value of shares, conversion of loans into shares and profits on shares transferred from one company to another would be subject to a capital gains tax.[264]
(iii) Profits of companies would be subject to a progressive rate of company taxation, which would be levied relative to the amount of

---

253 D. Pallister, S. Stewart, I. Lepper, *op.cit.*, 62. R162 million (£81 million) flowed out of the country and Anglo American along with many of the life assurance companies were able to buy up these shares at fire sale prices.
254 *Hoek Verslag, op.cit.*, 14.
255 *Ibid.*, 15.
256 *Ibid.*, 15.
257 *Ibid.*, 16.
258 *Ibid.*, 16.
259 *Ibid.*, 17.
260 *Ibid.*, 17-18.
261 *Ibid*, 20.
262 *Ibid.*, 23.
263 *Ibid.*, 23.
264 *Ibid.*, 24.

(iv)	Increase in Non-Resident Shareholders Tax from the then current 15%.[266]
(v)	Monetary operations of investment companies should fall under the Banks Act.[267]
(vi)	Excess cash should be invested in government bonds.[268]
(vii)	Establishment of large Government corporations, which rely on private initiative and are financed by financial institutions.[269]
(viii)	Development of homelands and border industries. Bantu Investment Corporation to be replaced by the Bantu Homelands Development Finance Corporation.[270]
(ix)	Any company producing more than 15% of a strategic commodity, such as coal (35%) and gold (38%) in the case of Anglo American, must have a South African board of directors, 50% of whom must be nominated by government.[271]
(x)	The nationality of directors would have to be disclosed, as well as the principals of all nominees and the names of all companies and institutions involved in contracts of control.[272]

paid up capital plus shareholders' premium.[265]

Dr. Verwoerd saw the first draft of the Hoek report at the end of 1965. It was subsequently revised in 1968. In a private interview recorded by the leader of the Herstigte Nasionale Party two months before he died, Prof. Hoek disclosed that this revised report was stolen from his safe at his offices in Pretoria. He also revealed that General van den Bergh was his next door neighbour. Notwithstanding that the first report states on the front page that it was written for Dr. Verwoerd, Prof. Hoek inferred that Dr. Verwoerd may not have seen it. Clearly enormous pressure had been exerted on Prof. Hoek to remain silent about the whole matter.

On 25 January 1966 Dr. Verwoerd referred to the report during his speech at the opening of parliament and fired another warning shot in Mr. Oppenheimer's direction when he said: "We shall fight the concentrations of power and monopolies which are present in our country and are a fundamental danger".[273] The implications for the Oppenheimer empire were dire, for if the Hoek proposals had been implemented, Anglo American's extensive powers would have been severely curtailed. What was bad for Anglo American would thus only have been good for South Africa.

---

265 *Ibid.*, 24.
266 *Ibid.*, 24.
267 *Ibid.*, 26.
268 *Ibid.*, 27.
269 *Ibid.*, 28.
270 *Ibid.*, 31.
271 *Ibid.*, 32.
272 *Ibid.*, 34.
273 J.A. Marais, *op cit.*, 184.

Professor Piet Hoek, whose astounding revelations about Anglo American Corporation may have changed the course of South African history, if his recommendations had been adopted by Dr. Verwoerd.

Shortly after Dr. Verwoerd's assassination, his successor, Balthazar Johannes Vorster, warned Professor Hoek not to make his report public as it could cause him embarrassment, and eventually all circulation of the report was forbidden.[274] This does not come as a surprise, as by this time Harry Oppenheimer had developed "cordial relations with Vorster".[275]

SOUTH AFRICAN RESERVE BANK[276]

There have been occasional rumours that Dr. Verwoerd was planning to reform the South African Reserve Bank. However, the author has yet to find any credible evidence to support such an allegation, except for the brief mention of the establishment of a State Bank, as part of the policies of the *Herenigde Nasionale Party* in an editorial of *Die Transvaler* of 27 March 1941. However, he can report the following:

In February 1990 the author was introduced by a neighbour of his, Moyna Traill-Smith,[277] to Mrs. Judy Wolman who resided in Lakeside, a suburb of Cape Town. Mrs. Wolman said that in early 1966 she had a private meeting with Dr. Verwoerd at his office in Cape Town. She told him all about the fraudulent banking monopoly, which creates money out of nothing as a debt and enslaves everyone through usury, and how this system was undermining South Africa. Dr. Verwoerd was enthralled with what Mrs. Wolman had to say and asked her to return for a further discussion. This meeting never took place as Dr. Verwoerd was murdered. This newly created awareness of the central problem for mankind for at least the last 300 years, namely the iniquitous operations of the central banking cartel, raises the intriguing prospect, that if Dr. Verwoerd had been able to act on this information before he was murdered, he would have reformed the SA Reserve Bank on state banking lines, and separate development and its associated freedoms would have succeeded and that Southern Africa would have benefitted enormously *in perpetuum*.

---

274 D. Pallister, S. Stewart, I. Lepper, *op.cit.*, 65-66.
275 *Ibid.*, 60. See also *Washington Observer Newsletter*, 15 January 1975, 1, where it is stated that "Vorster is supported by the subversive pro-communist, Harry Oppenheimer, the most powerful billionaire in Africa, the newspapers, the wealthy classes, the Jews and the Negro leaders who have been let in on the plan ... the Rockefeller-Rothschild-Oppenheimer plan to set up an economic super-government over the southern portion of the continent".
276 After the author was elected to the board of the SA Reserve Bank on 23 August 2003, Anglo American insisted on receiving a copy of his *curriculum vitae*.
277 Moyna Traill-Smith was the secretary of A.K. Chesterton, the founder of the League of Empire Loyalists in 1954 and the editor of *Candour* newsletter.

Chapter VII

SOME GENERAL OBSERVATIONS

Cabinet

Dr. Verwoerd had an incredible stamina and capacity for work. Cabinet meetings, held at the Union Buildings, started punctually at seven o'clock in the morning. He usually worked for sixteen hours a day, often eating only a sandwich for lunch. When he left his office, the boot of his ministerial car was filled with voliminous files for further work. Dr. Verwoerd had a prodigious memory and a microscopic knowledge and penchant for detail which enabled him to be such an effective minister.[278] With his superb intellect Dr. Verwoerd was able to dominate proceedings at cabinet meetings like no other leader before or after him. B.J. Vorster provides an example of what transpired at a meeting held in January 1961 to consider what the implications would be if South Africa should leave the Commonwealth. Dr. Verwoerd asked each cabinet member to prepare a memo about the ramifications for their departments, if such an event should take place. Dr. Verwoerd explained that by having all this information at their disposal, they would be able to reach a decision.

"At the meeting where this fateful decision had to be arrived at Dr. Verwoerd, very courteously called upon each minister, in order of seniority, to read his memo. He had a little notebook with him and from time to time he made short notes in it. When every member of the cabinet had delivered their memo's he said he would try to sum up this information at their disposal. Beginning with the memo delivered by the senior member he briefly summed it up, but then commented that unfortunately the honourable member's department had failed to include in to their memo this and that and the other which was also relevant to the issue.

"Mr. Vorster said this kind of comment was repeated after every one of the memo's had been summed up. The entire cabinet had become silent and overawed by this man who obviously knew more about their departments than they did themselves.[279]

---

[278] J. Botha, *op.cit.*, 33 and J.J. Scholtz, *op.cit.*, 82.
[279] P.C. Swanepoel, *op.cit.*, 59-60. See also *Verwoerd só onthou ons hom, op.cit.,* 130, B. Fourie, Buitelandse Sake Onder Dr. Verwoerd, where Mr. Fourie writes, "I never considered him as someone who was dogmatic, who had only one idea in his head."

Parliament

Although the timbre of Dr. Verwoerd's voice did not produce a striking trajectory, with his height of 6ft. 2 inches, he nonetheless cut an impressive figure. His speeches were always well prepared and researched, yet he never used notes and was equally fluent in both English and Afrikaans.[280] Dr. Verwoerd could speak for hours, yet an examination of his speeches shows that not a single word or phrase used could be considered superfluous. A parliamentary reporter once remarked that:

> "To any student of human nature the sight of Dr. Verwoerd in oratorical action in the House of Assembly is fascinating. He speaks with all the confidence and assurance in the world. He tosses aside other people's arguments as if they were mere baubles of balderdash".[281]

Dr. Verwoerd always spoke in a calm and serene manner without having to resort to histrionics and without any trace of fanaticism. He never faltered, back-tracked or lost his concentration.[282] With his extraordinary irrefragable logic and intelligence Dr. Verwoerd could not be bested in debate;[283] he simply ground his opponents into dust.

In private conversation Dr. Verwoerd was always very polite and took great pains to put his interlocutor at ease.[284] He would willingly listen to other opinions, but if the arguments raised were weak, he would quickly terminate the conversation. Before making an important decision it was his habit to consult with the Governor-General and later State President C.R. Swart.[285]

Correspondence

Dr. Verwoerd received an enormous amount of mail both while he was a cabinet minister and prime minister. Letters of encouragement and advice were received. Farmers who needed assistance with their income tax, mine workers who were dissatisfied with their shifts, professors who required detailed information, students who sought clarification of what they had been told by their lecturers, were some of the people who wrote to him. There were also thousands upon thousands of letters received from Blacks who had questions and solicited his guidance and counsel.

---

280 J.J. Scholtz, *op.cit.*, 16.
281 *Sunday Tribune*, 4 December 1960.
282 J. Botha, *op.cit.*, 122.
283 F. Barnard, *op.cit.*, 23.
284 J. Botha, *op.cit.*, 120.
285 *Verwoerd só onthou ons hom, op.cit.*, 184-185 T. Viljoen, Rondom Loskopdam.

Dr. Verwoerd and his wife Betsie at the prime minister's residence, Groote Schuur, 13 June 1959.

Many letters were also received from overseas, some of which were of a negative nature and came in particular from Sweden, the Soviet Union and the United States. All letters were read and received a reply in the finest detail.[286] Frequently Dr. Verwoerd would introduce additional arguments which the letter writer had not considered and would provide answers for these arguments, thus making his reply both convincing and watertight. (See Appendix I)

[286] F. Barnard, *op.cit.*, 149-150.

Dr. Verwoerd had a regular correspondent from Ghana who said that he often prayed for him. There were also correspondents from Nigeria, and a number of Black students whom Dr. Verwoerd assisted with their studies out of his own pocket.[287] Numerous letters were received from Negroes in the United States who wrote that they admired Dr. Verwoerd because he was honest and sincere. Their admiration was grounded in their belief that Dr. Verwoerd was the only White man who had ever done anything for Black people.[288]

LIFESTYLE

Dr. Verwoerd led a very modest lifestyle. When moving into a new office he would leave the furnishings unchanged, seeing no need to incur unnecessary state expenditure. Every year he travelled by train for the parliamentary sessions in Cape Town. Not only did this method of transport save the state money, but it enabled him to relax and catch up with his reading. It was his custom to greet all the personnel of the train right down to the bedding boy and at the end of the journey he would thank the engine driver.[289] Dr. Verwoerd never abused his position while in government. He always used his 1942 black Chrysler Windsor when attending political meetings in the 1950s and eschewed the use of a government vehicle.[290] When writing letters to private persons, he would purchase his own postage stamps.

Dr. Verwoerd only owned an unassuming cottage at Betty's Bay where he could pursue his favourite hobby, angling. Later he acquired a small farm[291] of 34 hectares (84 acres), he named Stokkiesdraai, on the banks of both sides of the Vaal river.[292] The farm was a donation from Messrs. Hennie du Toit and Marius Jooste, the managing directors of Voortrekkerpers Beperk and Afrikaanse Pers Beperk respectively, and was placed in a trust, in which Dr. Verwoerd was the usufructuary. Other gifts received included furniture, a herd of Jersey cows and a motor boat, *Smithfield*, which he used for fishing.[293] Dr. Verwoerd was an accomplished cabinet maker[294] and on other occasions wired the house of his parents in Brandfort, Orange Free State, with electricity, installed pipes for a warm water system and erected the roof of a cowshed at Stokkiesdraai.[295]

---

287 *Ibid.*, 151.
288 *Ibid.*, 150.
289 *Ibid.*, 157.
290 *Ibid.*, 25.
291 The property was held in trust for Dr. Verwoerd and his wife and on their death reverted back to the donors.
292 F. Barnard, *op.cit.*, 133.
293 A. Boshoff, *op.cit.*, 196.
294 *Ibid.*, 175.
295 J.J. Scholtz, *op.cit.*, 75.

Dr. Verwoerd with a 468 pound bluefin tuna which he caught in False Bay, Cape Town, from the Hare brothers' boat *Speranza* on 2 February 1964.

Although the Verwoerds had seven children, servants were never employed. Every year, shortly before Christmas, Dr. Verwoerd would give a dinner party for all the gardeners and labourers who were responsible for the maintenance of the gardens at Libertas, in the large dining room. Afterwards they would each be given a gift.[296]

---

296 F. Barnard, *op.cit.*, 157-158.

Chapter VIII

ASSASSINATION

On 30 July 1966 the *Rand Daily Mail* which was usually known for its hostile attitude towards Dr. Verwoerd, published the following glowing tribute.

"At the age of nearly 65 Dr. Verwoerd has reached the peak of a remarkable career. No other South African prime minister has ever been in such a powerful position in the country. He is at the head of a massive majority after a resounding victory at the polls. The nation is suffering from a surfeit of prosperity and he can command almost unlimited funds for all that he needs in the way of military defence. He can claim that South Africa is a shining example of peace in a troubled continent, if only because overwhelming domestic power can always demand peace. Finally, if that was not enough, he can face the session (of Parliament) with the knowledge that, short of an unthinkable show of force by people whom South Africans are rapidly being taught to regard as their enemies, he can snap his fingers at the United Nations. Thanks to the recent judgment of the Hague Court (on the South West Africa issue) he can afford to condescend to the world body graciously remaining a member as long as it suits him. Indeed, the Prime Minister has never had it so good!"

There was indeed a surfeit of prosperity. A Professor Gilbert from America described the performance of the South African economy as one of the miracles of modern science.[297] The Gross Domestic Product was growing at 7.9% per annum, while the Gross National Product increased during the period 1961-1966 by 30% - the so called "fabulous years".[298] Black unemployment had been reduced to an all time low of 5% and inflation stood at less than 2%. South Africa did not have any foreign loans. The living standards of Blacks were rising at 5.3% per annum, while those of Whites were increasing by 3.9% per annum. Almost the entire population was now adequately housed and fed and except for some areas in the homelands, poverty had been eradicated. The houses, clinics, hospitals, schools and universities, and recreation facilities, which were erected in Black areas, had all been built on Dr. Verwoerd's initiative[299] and paid for almost entirely by the White taxpayer. The vast majority

---

[297] J.A. Marais, *op.cit.*, 23.
[298] *Financial Mail*, 14 July 1966, 59.
[299] S.E.D. Brown, Dr. Verwoerd Puts S.A.'s Case, *The South African Observer*, April 1961, 9. In a speech given to the South Africa Club in London on 23 March 1961 Dr. Verwoerd said: "...South Africa has done and is doing more for the welfare of its non-White peoples than any other state in Africa. In fact it seems as if it is already being realized that the Asiatic nations, and even others in Europe or South America, fall behind, sometimes far behind, the achievements of South Africa in this respect with regard to her Bantu".

of Black people sincerely appreciated what Dr. Verwoerd was doing for them and were enjoying the highest standard of living in Africa.[300] Dr. Verwoerd's Bantu Education policy, which was based on strict discipline and was tailored to meet the needs of the African people, had revolutionised the learning process and resulted in Black South Africans having the highest literacy in Africa and a higher rate of literacy than in most other parts of the rest of the developing world. [301] On 3 September 1966 Dr. Verwoerd had made a breakthrough in meeting a foreign Black leader, the Prime Minster of Lesotho, Chief Leabua Jonathan, whose country was about to achieve independence on 4 October 1966. Both leaders deemed their meeting to have been a success.[302]

Why would anyone want to assassinate Dr. Verwoerd? Regrettably, there were a number of highly placed persons in the financial world who desired his demise, and more particularly the Rothschild banking dynasty. Dr. Verwoerd had crossed a number of red lines. He had created an autarkic state, paid back all South Africa's foreign loans and had designed a unique plan for the resolution of South Africa's racial problem.

There was also the strong possibility that he might reform the banking system. The international bankers needed to incorporate South Africa, with its treasure chest of minerals, into their planned New World Order whose principal objective is permanently to enslave mankind by means of perpetual debt and usury. Dr. Verwoerd, who had frequently declared that he would have nothing to do with such a satanic scheme, stood in their path and therefore had to be eliminated, even if it meant that violent means would have to be employed. The Rothschilds' local representative, Harry Oppenheimer, was an implacable foe of Dr. Verwoerd and as far back as 1955 in a parliamentary debate had asserted that "When you have a man prepared to slow down his nation's economic welfare on account of political theories, then you are dealing with an impractical fanatic".[303] The previous attempt to assassinate Dr. Verwoerd in April 1960 had failed by a hair breadth. In the interim Dr. Verwoerd's security under Colonel Carl (Callie) Richter had been considerably strengthened. A more ingenious and calculating plan would have to be devised, which necessitated the recruitment of an insider within Dr. Verwoerd's closest circle of associates.

---

300 *Verwoerd aan die Woord, op.cit.*, 515.
301 *Ibid.*, 515.
302 F. *Barnard, op.cit.*, 152.
303 J. Botha, *op.cit.*, 22.

B.J Vorster (left) at a banquet held in his honour by the South African Jewish Board of Deputies on 2 June 1976. When he was elected as prime minster on 13 September 1966, Vorster stated that "My road is to walk further along the one set by Hendrik Verwoerd. With God's help I will follow his path". Vorster did the exact reverse and slavishly followed the master plan, which was handed to him by the Rothschild influenced Council on Foreign Relations (See end note 311), and which resulted in the betrayal and enslavement of all South Africa's people.

BALTHAZAR JOHANNES VORSTER

In October 1958 at a meeting of a Freemason's Lodge in Johannesburg, Colonel Ernie Malherbe, head of Military Intelligence during the government of General Smuts (1939-1948), tipped off Harry Oppenheimer that one of his former agents, John Vorster, who had been used to penetrate the *Ossewa Brandwag* (Ox Wagon Sentinel) during World War II, had been appointed Deputy Minister of Education, Arts and Science and of Social Welfare and Pensions.[304] While studying law at the University of Stellenbosch during the years (1934-1938), John Vorster came under the influence of Professor William Mortimer Robertson Malherbe who was dean of the law faculty. "Mortie" Malherbe was a member of Freemason's Lodge and a liberal who had spent 14 years of his life in the Netherlands, where he was educated first at a Dutch school and later at the University of Leiden. Professor Malherbe had the habit of inviting his more intelligent students, one of whom

---

[304] P.J. Pretorius, *op.cit.*, 144. Vorster was the last male of 15 siblings and according to his youngest sister, Margaretha Johanna Vorster, was known as the 'spoiled baby' of the Vorster family. He suffered from low blood pressure and spent long hours sleeping. As a consequence thereof he read insufficiently and much of his thinking was provided by others. He once informed an uncle of the author, Rex S. Walker, the President of Westlake Golf Club, Lakeside, Cape Town that he played golf in order to reduce his high levels of "stress".

was Vorster, for walks in the surrounding mountains on Saturday afternoons, where they would discuss law, politics and current affairs.[305] At the relatively young age of 20 Vorster became a Freemason.[306]

In September 1937 Vorster was recruited as a police agent and spent the summer holidays of 1937-1938 in Pretoria being trained as an undercover agent for eventual infiltration of the *Ossewa Brandwag*. After his training Vorster received the large sum of £1,000 (R2,000)[307] to cover his future expenses. In early 1942 Vorster, who now held the rank of general in this subversive organisation, was "arrested" and spent the next two years at Pretoria Central Prison and an internment camp at Koffiefontein, Orange Free State. Throughout his incarceration in bungalow No. 10, which was dubbed 10 Downing Street, Vorster received food parcels and regular visits from Julius First.[308] First, who was treasurer of the South African Communist Party, was also the father-in-law of Joe Slovo who later organized the Communist revolution in South Africa on behalf of the international bankers in the 1980s and early 1990s.

On 23 July 1961 Dr. Verwoerd informed John Vorster that he had been appointed Minister of Justice. The following day Vorster communicated this news to Anton Rupert. Rupert asked Vorster to meet him at his home at the top of Thibault Street in Stellenbosch on 26 July 1961. At this meeting Rupert phoned Harry Oppenheimer and introduced Vorster to him. Oppenheimer was very pleased to hear that Vorster had received such an important position in the cabinet.[309] At about the same time Vorster was recruited by the Central Intelligence Agency (CIA), also known as "the company", and was promised the premiership at some future date. In September 1962 Vorster was drawn into the web of MI6.[310] In the meantime the liberal press built up an entirely false image of Vorster as a hardened right winger.

At six 'o clock on the evening of Monday, 27 July 1964 Vorster was asked to attend a meeting at Harry Oppenheimer's Brenthurst estate in Parktown, Johannesburg. Also present were Anton Rupert, Quintin Whyte, a CFR member and CIA agent, as well as an unknown representative of MI6. At this meeting which lasted two and a half hours, a plot to assassinate Dr. Verwoerd was discussed. Initially, Vorster balked at the idea, but because he had already compromised himself with his foreign intelligence connections, he eventually agreed. Once again Vorster was promised the premiership, but it was conditional on him following a blueprint which would slowly, but stealthily dismantle the apartheid structure and civilised White rule and then hand over

---

305 J. D'Oliviera, *Vorster - die Mens,* Perskor, 1977, Johannesburg, 23.
306 J.A. Marais, *op.cit.,* 143.
307 *Ibid.,* 143.
308 F. Richter, *Vlug Vir Die Strafgerig,* Libanon-Uitgewers, Mosselbaai, Western Cape, 1995, 122.
309 P.J. Pretorius, *op.cit.,* 145.
310 *Ibid.,* 145.

the country to a designated group of Black puppets.[311] Later that same evening Vorster summoned his head of the security police, General "Lang" Hendrik van den Bergh, to his official residence in Pretoria and forced him to become willy-nilly a participant in this abhorrent affair.[312]

THE ASSASSIN

Demetrio Mimikos Tsafendas was born in Lourenço Marques, Mozambique on 14 January 1918, the illegitimate offspring of a Cretan, Michaelatos Tsafendakis, and his half caste maid,[313] Amelia Williams, whose mother was a Swazi.[314] He spent the first six years of his life with his paternal grandmother in Alexandria, Egypt. From 1925 to 1927 he lived in Lourenço Marques and from 1927 to 1930 he attended an English medium primary school in Middelburg, Transvaal, where he was given the nickname "Blackie" because of his dark complexion, and passed Standard III. He then returned to Lourenço Marques and attended the Anglican Mission School from 1931 to 1933, whereafter he left school. Between 1935 and 1938 Tsafendas made three unsuccessful attempts to obtain permanent residence in South Africa. Notwithstanding these refusals Tsafendas entered South Africa illegally in 1938 and at about this time became a member of the South African Communist Party.[315] Tsafendas's communist leanings would provide a convenient cover "behind which others in Britain, the USA and probably also Israel, as well as some others in South Africa operated".[316] From 1940 to 1942 he worked as a welder at the British Mining Supply Co. (Pty) Ltd in Faraday Street, Johannesburg.[317]

Between 1942 and 1947 Tsafendas obtained casual employment as a seaman/ steward on *Liberty* cargo ships and at the same time made several unsuccessful further attempts to settle in the United States permanently. During this time frame he was treated at three mental institutions for psychoneurosis, but according to the last hospital he stayed at, the North Grafton State Hospital

---

311 J.A. Marais, *op.cit.*, 181-182. This blue print or master plan contained four objectives:
  (i) The South African policy of White domination would have to be moderated in order to comply with some of the world's criticism and to prevent racial friction and possible bloodshed.
  (ii) Adaptations would have to be reasonably acceptable to the White voter, if the National Party was to remain in power.
  (iii) The execution of the plan must be concentrated in the political power structure of the country and may not clash with economic development and prosperity.
  (iv) It must satisfy Afrikaner nationalism, the English financier and industrialist and must ensure South Africa's defence and national security.
312 P.J. Pretorius, *op.cit.*, 159-160. According to S.E.D. Brown, who knew General van den Bergh well, the local representative of the CIA, William Rourke "Big Bill" Jordan, assisted van den Bergh with his farming operations outside Pretoria on a part time basis.
313 http://www.celebritymemorials.com/wordpress/dimitri-tsafendas/
314 *Verslag van die Kommissie van Ondersoek na die Dood van wyle Sy Edele dr. Hendrik Frensch Verwoerd*, Bienedell Uitgewers, Pretoria, 2000, 6-7.
315 *Ibid.*, 12.
316 J.A. Marais, *The Founders of the New South Africa*, pamphlet, Pretoria, 15 July 1994, 21.
317 *Verslag, op.cit.*, 19-20.

in Massachusetts, "he faked mental illness because he was afraid to ship out because of the numerous leakings of ships".[318] From 1947-1959 Tsafendas wandered around Europe. He also made numerous further attempts to settle in South Africa, but on 1 September 1959 he was finally placed on a blacklist of prohibited immigrants.[319]

As stated by Advocate Pretorius, Tsafendas worked at Anton Rupert's Rembrandt Tobacco cigarette factory, a subsidiary of Rothmans International, from July 1960 to January 1962.[320] On one occasion Tsafendas informed workers at the factory that he would kill Dr. Verwoerd if he could find an opportunity. Rupert never spoke to Tsafendas, but after he became unemployed supported him financially.[321]

At a secret meeting in March 1963 held in Birmingham, England at which Anton Rupert and members of the CFR, CIA[322] and MI6 were present, it was formally agreed that Dr. Verwoerd would be assassinated and that Tsafendas would be trained and paid for that purpose.[323] While Rupert was the driving force behind Dr. Verwoerd's assassination, it was Rothschild who was the architect.[324] In July 1963 Tsafendas received weapons training by an anatomist who was experienced in the use of knives and where in all likelihood cadavers[325] were used for practice, at Kérkyra, the capital of the island of Corfu, off the west coast of Greece.[326] Thereafter Tsafendas proceeded to Brighton Mental Hospital, England where he was brainwashed by means of hypnosis by the same Dr. Solly Jacobson, who had previously brainwashed David Pratt in order to assassinate Dr. Verwoerd in April 1960.[327] This treatment took place shortly after Jacobson fled from South Africa in the middle of July 1963 in the wake of the arrests of many of his Jewish co-conspirators at the Lilliesleaf farm in Rivonia.[328] Jacobson employed the brainwashing techniques of the CIA's MK-Ultra programme,[329]

---

318 *Ibid.*, 18. The report was dated 12 December 1946.
319 *Ibid.*, 25.
320 P.J. Pretorius, *op.cit.*, 157.
321 *Ibid.*, 157.
322 *Ibid.*, 157.
323 *Ibid.*, 157.
324 *Ibid.*, 161.
325 A. Bird, *op.cit.*, 213 and J.A. Marais, *op.cit.*, 205.
326 P.J. Pretorius, *op.cit.*, 157.
327 A. Bird, *op.cit.*, 213-215.
328 *Ibid.*, 210-211.
329 MK means that the programme was developed by the Technical Services Staff of the CIA and Ultra indicates most secret. The programme was initially under the direction of Dr. Sidney Gottlieb. The CIA's Scientific Intelligence Division organised the project in co-ordination with the Special Operations Division of the U.S. Army's Chemical Corps. The purpose of this project was to develop biological, chemical and radiological materials with which to control human behaviour in clandestine operations. The project operated from 1953-1973. D.W. Michaels, *The Barnes Review*, John F. Kennedy's Battle with the CIA: 1961-1963, Vol. XXII No. 1, Washington D.C., January/February 2016, 22-28. See also T.M. Silver, *Lifting The Veil An Investigative History of the United States Pathocracy*, Chap. V MK-ULTRA for details of how unbalanced, but not mad persons, such as Tsafendas, were coached into committing murders. http://www.wanttoknow.info/mk/liftingtheveil#5

and used the sign of the assegaai[330] and drops of blood which would be deployed later to activate Tsafendas to commit a murder at some time in the future.

After Solly Jacobson fled South Africa, his former partner, Allan Bird began to see him "in a more sinister light, no longer as an altruistic, starry-eyed worker for freedom, but as an international terrorist, aiming with his consorts to conquer the world".[331]

During 1964 Dr. Bird met General van den Bergh in order to discuss his deep concerns about Jacobson. Van den Bergh listened attentively, but pointed out that everything Dr. Bird said was "speculative", but admitted that "Jacobson's activities aroused suspicion".[332] The matter for now obvious reasons was not pursued, even though pursuit of it may well have saved Dr. Verwoerd's life.

In 1966 after Dr. Verwoerd's assassination Dr. Bird visited Brigadier Johan Coetzee who was head of the Security Police and informed him of his suspicions that Dr. Jacobson may have treated Tsafendas at Brighton Mental Hospital. Coetzee agreed with Dr. Bird's suspicions and undertook to have the matter investigated, but nothing further transpired. On 24 December 1979 Dr. Bird visited Brigadier Coetzee about another matter, whereupon Coetzee volunteered the following information that "it had been established that Tsafendas was in fact treated by Jacobson, immediately before his departure for South Africa" in 1963. Dr. Bird continues: "However there was not sufficient evidence to have Dr. Jacobson extradited. 'If he were in the country it might be possible to open a case against him,' he said. This evasiveness was baffling and irritating in the extreme. One got the impression that at the top it had been decided to liquidate and leave hanging in mid-air the whole sequence of circumstantial evidence about Jacobson". Coetzee had once written a book on the life of Trotsky and spoke fluent Hebrew. He was a personal friend of General Yitzhak Hofi director of the Mossad and was well disposed towards the Israelis.[333] Was he perhaps a double agent?

To continue with Tsafendas's peregrinations, on 4 November 1963 he entered South Africa by motor car at the Komatipoort border post on a Portuguese passport with a temporary residence permit, notwithstanding the fact that he was a prohibited immigrant.[334] The following month he obtained employment at City Engineers and Carron Ltd in Johannesburg and remained there until he was dismissed on 3 February 1964.[335] Four days later he found a job at F.A. Poole (Pty) Ltd and stayed there until 10 July 1964 when he was sacked by the

---

330 This was also the symbol of the ANC's military wing, the Spear of the Nation.
331 A. Bird, *op.cit.*, 212.
332 *Ibid.*, 312.
333 *Ibid.*, 212-214.
334 *Verslag, op.cit.*, 26.
335 *Ibid.*, 28.

manager, Mr. Vercuiel, because he was being disruptive amongst his fellow workers and for his poor workmanship. When he left, Tsafendas made the following threat: "You are just like your bloody Government. I will get you. I will also get your Prime Minister".[336] Tsafendas then allegedly travelled around Rhodesia, where he had a sister, and Mozambique for the next eight months. During this period Tsafendas visited the Greek consul in Lourenço Marques and mentioned that he had received R5,000 (£2,500)[337] from his family[338] in Pretoria. This is the sum[339] which Tsafendas is believed to have been paid in order to assassinate Dr. Verwoerd. On 11 March 1965 he arrived in Durban on the *S.S. Karanga*, a cargo-passenger ship of the British India Steam Navigation Company. The immigration officials at the port failed to identify Tsafendas as being a prohibited immigrant, as the surname he had given and which appeared on the passenger list was Tsafendar.[340]

Between 21 June and 24 August 1965 Tsafendas resided at the Durban Men's Home. During this period he was observed by a Mrs. Theron,[341] the wife of a Durban lawyer, visiting the offices of an attorney, Rowley Israel Arenstein, who was a self-confessed communist,[342] on at least two occasions. Tsafendas allegedly wished to purchase a translation bureau, but nothing came of these negotiations with Arenstein.

Meanwhile the *modus operandi* for the assassination of Dr. Verwoerd was being discussed at higher levels. According to Advocate Pretorius, in February 1965 B.J. Vorster arrived at the idea that the best time to assassinate Dr. Verwoerd would be after lunch, shortly before the afternoon sitting began at 2.15 pm, when in an unguarded and relaxed mood the members were walking about and talking to each other or paging through their documents.[343]

---

336 *Ibid.*, 30.
337 £2,500 was worth £43,664 in 2015.
  http://www.bankofengland.co.uk/education/Pages/resources/inflationtools/calculator/flash/default.aspx
338 *Verslag, op.cit.*, 33.
339 P.J. Pretorius, *op.cit.*, 160. Advocate Pretorius provides a different timeline and states that on 9 June 1965 at 9.30pm Tsafendas was paid R5,000 to commit the murder. He was paid by an unknown MI6 agent who had been driven in a car owned by Anton Rupert. Rupert was not present, but his driver, who did not know what the transaction was about, had driven the vehicle. It needs to be stressed that a large portion of the information regarding Tsafendas's *curriculum vitae* was provided by himself and cannot be relied upon either for accuracy or honesty.
340 *Verslag, op.cit.*, 33.
341 *Ibid.*, 36.
342 B. Temkin, *op.cit.*, 32.
343 P.J. Pretorius, *op.cit.*, 160.

During the period 27 July to 6 August 1965, Vorster's personal representative and Chief of the Security Police, Hendrik van den Bergh, attended meetings with members of the CIA,[344] CFR and MI6. One of the CFR members, Henry Kissinger, who was at that time an adviser to Nelson Rockefeller, attended a meeting where a progress report on the planned assassination of Dr. Verwoerd was submitted and elaborated on. Methods of how the assassination should be covered up were also discussed.[345]

On 28 August 1965 Tsafendas arrived in Cape Town, and was employed in a number of short term occupations, until he applied for the position of temporary messenger at the Houses of Parliament at the beginning of July 1966. On 18 July 1966 Tsafendas was interviewed by the chief messenger, Mr. Burger, and two senior messengers. He was not required to fill in an application form and he was not subjected to any form of character or police checks,[346] such as fingerprinting, which could have been used to establish if he had a criminal record or was *persona non grata*.[347] He lied to the chief messenger that he was a White South African citizen and in possession of a South African identity card. Tsafendas was unable to produce an identity card, but instead showed a document with an identity number which corresponded with an identity number on his unemployment insurance card.[348] It was also a requirement that a messenger be bilingual in both English and Afrikaans, but Tsafendas could only speak broken Afrikaans.[349] Two days later on 20 July 1966 Tsafendas was informed that he had been appointed a temporary messenger with effect from 1 August 1966. This entitled him to wear the navy blue uniform with green piping of a messenger.[350]

On 30 August 1965 Tsafendas had made an application [351] to the Regional Representative of the Population Register in Cape Town to be classified as a Coloured person so that he could marry a coloured girl, Miss Helen Daniels.[352] His application was refused and on 9 August 1966 the Minister of Internal Affairs, P.M.K. le Roux signed a deportation order for Tsafendas's expulsion from South Africa. Due to various administrative delays caused in all probability by Vorster[353] as well as office inefficiencies, the minister's warrant was only typed in a letter on 1 September 1966, but by 6 September 1966 it had still not been delivered to the police.[354]

---

344 *Ibid.*, 160.
345 *Ibid.*, 160.
346 *Verslag, op.cit.*, 100-101.
347 J.J.J. Scholtz. *op.cit.*, 136-137. In 1962 Major S.J. Venter, who was responsible for the security of parliament, recommended, after a number of thefts had taken place, that all employees obtain a police clearance certificate. This recommendation was not followed up because it took about four months to obtain such a certificate.
348 *Verslag, op.cit.*, 104.
349 *Ibid.*, 105.
350 *Ibid.*, 46. See also J. Basson, *"Meneer die Speaker!" Uit die Politieke Plakboek van Japie Basson* Politika, Kaapstad, 2012, 114 where Basson mentions that after the National Party came to power, the Coloured workers and cleaners were gradually phased out, and created the problem of finding sufficient white workers to do this underpaid work for the limited period of a parliamentary session which usually lasted for five months.
351 Verslag, *op.cit.*, 37-38.
352 *Ibid.*, 36.
353 P.J. Pretorius, *op.cit.*, 163.
354 *Verslag, op.cit.*, 95.

Dr. Allan V. Bird, the Johannesburg neurologist, who revealed in his autobiography that his partner, Solly Jacobson, coached both David Pratt and Demetrio Tsafendas to murder Dr. Verwoerd. (Photograph taken in Pretoria, August 1975 by Dr. Ingram Anderson, who was Dr. Verwoerd's personal physician, 9-10 April 1960, while he was being treated at the Johannesburg General Hospital).

In the 26 August 1966 South African edition of *TIME* magazine there appeared on the front page the trigger symbol of an assegaai and two drops of blood[355] on the right hand side of Dr. Verwoerd's face. On the back cover there was an advertisement for one of Anton Rupert's cigarette companies, Rothmans International. Inside the magazine there was a six page article entitled "SOUTH AFRICA: Delusions of Apartheid" and on the margins there appeared the heading "Murder in the Heart".

The extract reads as follows. Murder in the Heart. On the surface, many Africans seem to be happy enough about apartheid. "We know what we have is ours, even if it is the gift of the white boss," says Ephraim Tchabalata, who has grown rich on a chain of dry-cleaning establishments and filling stations. The streets of the cities echo with the laughter of Africans, and the townships rock to the Beatle beat of guitars, strummed by young men wearing the cowboy hats that have become the latest rage. But all too often the smiles hide resentment. Says one African: "If I walk in the streets of Johannesburg and a white man kicks me, I will grin and say, 'Baas, you would have made a great soccer player.' But there is murder in my heart. I wear different masks for different white people all the time." [The third and second last sentences bear all the hallmarks of having been concocted by an inventive journalist. Whites have never gone around kicking

---

355 J.A. Marais, *op.cit.*, 172.

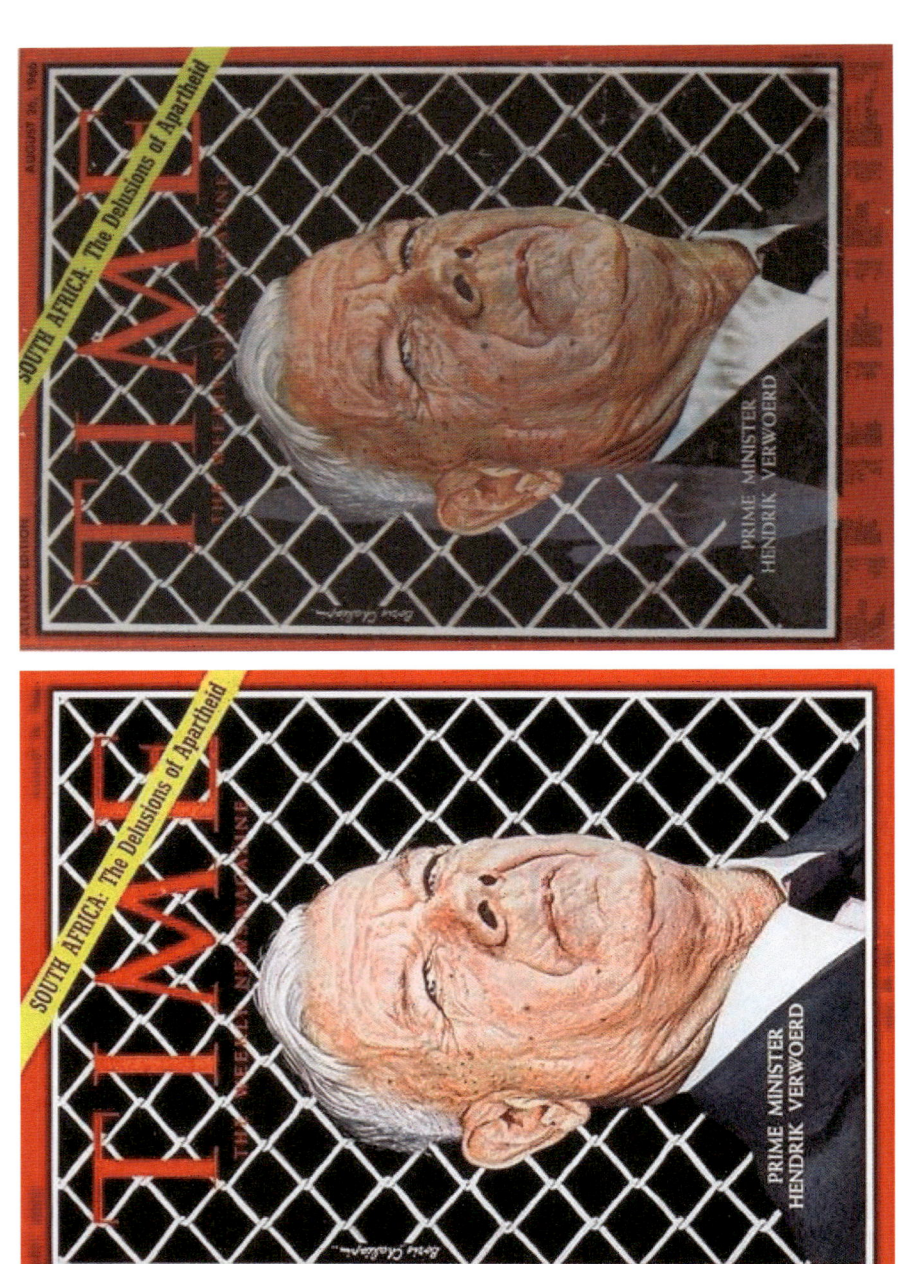

TIME magazine of 26 August 1966 carried a tendentious six page article on "apartheid" South Africa. On the cover Dr. Verwoerd's face has been given a haughty mien, while his skin has been doctored with heavy lining to make him appear forbidding, if not grotesque. In reality he had a smooth skin and often bore a genial smile. The background fencing was presumably intended to create the impression that South Africa was a concentration camp. The left hand cover was used for the international edition, while the right hand one was used for the South African issue. On the left of the latter cover there is a symbol of an assegaai blade and two drops of blood, which were probably intended to trigger the psychiatrically hypnotised Tsafendas into murdering Dr. Verwoerd.

Two days later there appeared in a front page article in *The Sunday Tribune*, published in Durban, under the headline CAPE NATS BACK ANTON RUPERT 'Verwoerd must go' plan. Written by Aida Parker, the first paragraph reads as follows:

"The knives are out in the Nationalist Party. Dr. Verwoerd faces his most serious split his Party has known since it came to power in 1948 – and Dr. Verwoerd himself is the target. There is now a planned operation to isolate Dr. Verwoerd and force a showdown. This tactic is to split the northern line by creating suspicion and unrest amongst them and in such a manner so as to isolate Dr. Verwoerd".

The circle of Cape Nats to whom the journalist referred, included the editors of *Die Burger* and *Die Beeld*, Piet Cillié and Schalk Pienaar respectively; businessmen A. D. Wassenaar of Sanlam and Jan S. Marais of Trust Bank; Dominee W.A. Landman of the NG Kerk, and Stellenbosch Professors Nic Olivier and Johan Degenaar.[357] This article was undoubtedly planted by the Rothschild/Oppenheimer/Rupert partnership in a fatuous attempt to unseat Dr. Verwoerd, but it made no impact, as his position, both in the National Party and in the country, was unassailable. However, it did serve to condition the public psychologically as to what was about to happen on a physical plane.

Every morning the messengers were searched on entering the parliamentary buildings, but not thereafter. Immediately after reporting for work on 6 September 1966, Tsafendas slipped out and went to William Rawbone & Company on the corner of Long and Castle Streets and purchased a razor sharp knife for R3.30 (£1.65). He then went to City Guns (Pty) Ltd in Hout Street and bought another knife. Both these knives were sold, notwithstanding the fact that it is a statutory offence to sell a knife longer than 3½ inches, unless the purchaser can provide valid reasons that such a knife is needed for a legitimate purpose. Neither Mr. Klein nor Mr. Harrison, the respective proprietors, was aware of this legislation.[358]

Blacks for the fun of it.] Another paragraph in the article included the following provocative statement: "A Greek immigrant from Cyprus was nearly refused entrance to South Africa recently because he had acquired a deep suntan on the ship".

According to Mrs. Joan Leonhardt, widow of parliamentary journalist of the South African Broadcasting Corporation, Carel Leonhardt, Tsafendas saw this issue of *TIME* magazine on the coffee table in the media office and asked if he could borrow it, which he duly did. She still has the magazine in her possession.[356]

---
356 http://censorbugbear-reports.blogspot.co.za/2011/05/boers-murdered-attacked-when-things-go.html
357 In 1972 Professor Degenaar assisted the author in writing a monograph on Albert Camus's *La Chute* (The Fall).
358 J.J.J. Scholtz. *op.cit.*, 10-11.

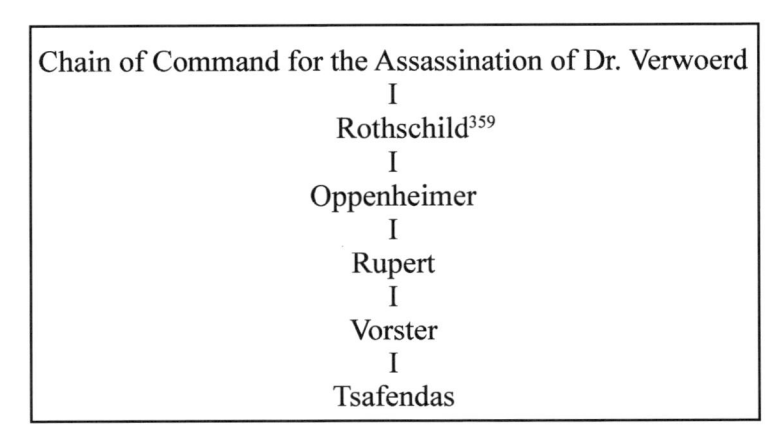

> Chain of Command for the Assassination of Dr. Verwoerd
> I
> Rothschild[359]
> I
> Oppenheimer
> I
> Rupert
> I
> Vorster
> I
> Tsafendas

These conspirators were assisted by the CIA, MI6, M-Apparatus of the Soviet Naval Espionage Service and rogue elements in the South African Department of Justice and the security police. Recently released, but redacted document, CIA-RDP79T00936A0047001170001-7, confirms the CIA's clandestine role in the assassination.

At 2.14pm, notwithstanding the fact that only messengers with the retired rank of colonel and above were allowed in the chamber, Tsafendas entered it from the end which is opposite to the Speaker's table, and walked briskly alongside the government benches, as if he had to deliver an urgent message. When he reached Dr. Verwoerd's bench, he dived on to him making it appear as if he had slipped and then stood up on his feet next to him, unsheathed his knife and stabbed him four times. The first stab struck Dr. Verwoerd's neck forcing him to raise his hands which then left his heart exposed. The second stab penetrated his aorta and the third and fourth stabs entered his

---

[359] The Rothschild connection may be explained as follows. C.J. Rhodes was backed by the Rothschild banking syndicate in establishing complete control over the diamond mines with the incorporation of De Beers Consolidated Mines Ltd on 12 March 1888 and was appointed chairman. In 1892 C.J. Rhodes was appointed chairman of the renamed Consolidated Goldfields Ltd which housed all of the Rothschild gold mines. The principal shareholder was Lord Nathan Rothschild who also owned a share of the British South Africa Company which operated in Rhodesia and was under the managing directorship of C.J. Rhodes. When C.J. Rhodes died on 26 March 1902 he was succeeded by Ernest Oppenheimer who arrived in South Africa in 1902. In 1917 together with JP Morgan & Co., a Rothschild controlled bank, Oppenheimer established Anglo American Corporation Ltd, which was set up to house the Rothschild's diamond and gold mines. Later this corporation expanded into holding major investments in commerce, finance and industry. From 1948 onwards it used its enormous financial power to interfere increasingly in South African politics in order to advance its commercial interests and the political agenda of the Rothschilds. On his death on 25 November 1957, Ernest Oppenheimer was succeeded by his son Harry. In 1999 Anglo American moved its headquarters to London. On 19 August 2000 Harry Oppenheimer died. Although the Oppenheimers no longer occupy any positions of prominence, they continue to exercise clandestine control through organisations such as the Illuminati "Committee of 300" of which Nicholas Frederick Oppenheimer is a member. See H.R. Abercrombie, *The Secret History of South Africa or Sixty five years in Transvaal*, Central News Agency Ltd, Johannesburg, 1952, 205. When Ewald Esselen, Attorney General of the ZAR, asked Rhodes why he did not cut diamonds in South Africa, the latter replied: "This is one of the things my masters, the Rothschilds, will not let me do".

lungs. Each of the last three wounds was of a fatal nature.[360] Dr. Ephraim Fisher, an opposition MP and a medical doctor, sitting diagonally opposite Dr. Verwoerd later stated that: "It is obvious that the assassin must have received training in how to wield a knife. Every time the knife slipped in between ribs and not across as an ordinary assailant would have done".[361]

Attempts were made to resuscitate Dr. Verwoerd, but within three minutes he was dead. As Dr. Verwoerd was being carried out of the chamber on a stretcher, Mr. Willie Olivier, Dr. Verwoerd's recently appointed private secretary, witnessed something very strange. Standing at the entrance, in a prominent position, was B.J. Vorster in an exceptionally emotional state howling crocodile tears[362] of grief – something which was irreconcilable with his usually austere image and behaviour. About the same time future prime minister P.W. Botha crossed the floor and wagged his finger furiously at Helen Suzman, the sole representative of the Progressive Party and said: "It's you who did this. It's all you liberals. You incite people. Now we will get you. We will get the lot of you".[363]

Dr. Verwoerd's funeral took place on 10 September 1966 in Pretoria. Over 250,000 people of all races and tribes packed the pavements as Dr. Verwoerd's hearse and cortege were driven through the streets to his burial place at the Hero's Acre. Most Whites stood in mute grief, but there were anguished cries and loud tears from other onlookers, all realising the loss that they had suffered.

The Cover-Up

Within half an hour of Dr. Verwoerd's murder, prior to an emergency cabinet meeting, B.J Vorster, who was still Minister of Justice, Police and Prisons informed Minister of Defence, P.W. Botha, that "This was a one man job". (See Appendix III). The following day Vorster made another false statement when he said that "the report that the Security Police have a file on Tsafendas is devoid of all truth".[364] About a week later it was revealed that there were in fact four files on Tsafendas – one had been lost, two had been destroyed (one of them without authority) and one was extant.[365]

---

360 J.J.J. Scholtz. *op.cit.*, Chap. 3, In *'n Ommesientjie* (In a Flash), 19-36.
361 J.A. Marais, *op.cit.*, 205.
362 *Ibid.*, 196. It is not entirely clear as to whether Vorster was seated in the chamber at the time of the assassination - J.J. Scholtz, a prominent Afrikaner liberal, writes that he was there – whereas journalists in the press gallery distinctly recall Vorster's wife, Tini, leaving the public gallery and then running down the passage to his office exclaiming excitedly: *"Pa, ons het hom, ons het hom !"* (Pa, we've got him, we've got him!).
363 H. Suzman, *In No Uncertain Terms*, Jonathan Ball Publishers, Johannesburg, 1993, 69. On 18 January 1989 President P.W. Botha suffered a "stroke", whereas it was in fact an attempted assassination caused by his tea being poisoned. Information provided to the author by his widow, Barbara Botha.
364 J.A. Marais, *op.cit.*, 189-190.
365 *Ibid.*, 190. In 1994 the entire archive of the South African Police was deliberately destroyed.

For 48 hours Hendrik van den Bergh interrogated Tsafendas intensively in order to establish exactly what he knew about the whole conspiracy, and which participants and international links he might disclose if he should be placed under cross examination in a trial.[366] Not surprisingly Van den Bergh came to the same conclusion as Vorster, that it was a one man job and also that Tsafendas was not responsible for his actions, even though he was not medically qualified to make such an assertion.[367] As Jaap Marais, who sat in the fourth row directly behind Dr. Verwoerd in the chamber, has stated, the lone assassin hypothesis is "palpable nonsense".[368] A pre-trial hearing was held in the Supreme Court, Cape Town from 17-20 October 1966 and was presided over by the Judge President of the Cape of Good Hope Division, Andries Beyers.[369] The attorney who defended Tsafendas, was David Bloomberg[370] of the firm Bloomberg, Baigel and Company. The psychiatrists led by Doctors Isaac Sakinofsky, Ralph Kossew and Abraham Zabow who testified on Tsafendas' behalf *pro deo*, as well as one of the assessors sitting on the bench, who was also a psychiatrist, were unanimous in their decision that Tsafendas suffered from schizophrenia and was therefore insane and not fit to stand trial.[371] No counter evidence was called for. Justice Beyers did not allow himself any time to reflect and reserve judgement in such an important case and promptly followed the advice of the psychiatrists. Yet how could a madman have planned and executed such a complicated murder all by himself? We must thus assume that Tsafendas experienced numerous *lucida intervalla*, but the psychiatrists did not make any reference to such normal states of mind which would have enabled him to pursue his criminal activities. When Tsafendas committed the murder he did not display any signs of disorientation, which have always been a classic symptom of insanity. During the last 25 years of his life Tsafendas had managed to visit a similar number of countries – something which an insane person is most unlikely to have accomplished.

Particular emphasis was placed on Tsafendas's belief that a tapeworm had influenced his decision to assassinate Dr. Verwoerd. As a teenager Tsafendas had suffered from a tape worm which was successfully removed,[372] but this

---

366 P.J. Pretorius, *op.cit.*, 164. N. Pnematicatos, *It's Not All Greek: Neoklis' Fish Hoek,* Zip Print, Cape Town, 2004, 135 writes that Tsafendas visited him a few months before the assassination. He reported the visit to the Security Police who stated that they were already aware of the visit. This constant surveillance reinforces the presumption that Tsafendas was a CIA asset under the protection of General van den Bergh.
367 *Ibid.*, 164.
368 J.A. Marais, *The Founders of the New South Africa*, pamphlet, Pretoria, 15 July 1994, 16.
369 J.J.J. Scholtz. *op.cit.*, 76. In 1928 Dr. Verwoerd told Judge Beyers, who was at that time a lecturer in law at the University of Stellenbosch, in all seriousness, "I am going to become prime minister".
370 Bloomberg was later involved in a R2 million bribery scandal with casino boss, Sol Kerzner, and the premier of the Transkei, Chief George Matanzima. Allegations of bribery, corruption, fraud and perjury were later withdrawn because the National Party government refused to extradite Kerzner and Bloomberg to the Transkei. http://www.anc.org.za/caucus/show.php?ID=345
371 J.J.J. Scholtz, Chap. 9, *Die Verhaal van die Lintwurm* (The Tale of the Tapeworm), 96-111.
372 *Ibid.*, 102.

fear of an imaginary tape worm was in all likelihood suggested by his handlers in order to improve his prospects of being declared insane. Tsafendas had an IQ of 125[373] and such dissembling was well within his capabilities. In his prison file, A5078, Tsafendas was described as being "exceptionally inventive and a cunning individual who is both physically and mentally capable of planning and executing an escape".[374]

Much of the evidence points in the other direction and indicates that Tsafendas, although vulnerable to manipulation through hypnosis on account of his unstable character and inferiority complex, principally because of his half caste status, was indeed sane.[375] For example in April 1966 while staying in the same room at a house in Milton Road, Observatory with a Mr. Bornman, the latter stated that Tsafendas did not show any signs of being mentally disturbed,[376] while a Mr. Hartford, a reporter from the *Cape Argus*, who interviewed Tsafendas in July 1966, said that Tsafendas seemed to be quite normal and that he had no reason to believe that he was mentally disturbed.[377] It has already been observed that Tsafendas faked being mentally ill in order to stay in the United States in 1947. In 1972 a psychologist, Dr. Willie Visser, was reported as saying: "Dimitri Tsfendas murdered the late Dr. H.F. Verwoerd after being subjected to intensive brainwashing and strong hypnotic suggestions".[378] This does not mean that Tsafendas was insane in terms of the Mental Disorders Act. Anyone who watches television, and in particular advertisements and newscasts, on a regular basis exposes him- or herself to a softer form of brainwashing or autosuggestion, whereby the prefrontal and association area of the cortex are dominated by the television screen. This constant visual stimulus fixates the viewer and causes habituation of response. The left cortical hemisphere, which is the centre of visual and calculating processes, ceases to function and is reduced merely to tracking the images on the screen. In the long term, the influence of what is seen and heard on television applies almost as much to press headlines and the harangues of street demagogues.

The *Commission of Enquiry into the Circumstances of the Death of the late the Honourable Dr. Hendrik Frensch Verwoerd* was set up under Justice Theo van Wyk who had previously served as South Africa's *ad hoc* judge at the

---

373 *Ibid.*, 100.
374 J.A. Marais, *op.cit.*, 208.
375 Some prison letters of Tsafendas may be found in Z. Adams, *Demetrios Tsafendas Race, Madness and the Archive,* Dissertation, University of the Western Cape, December 2011. Many of the letters are well written and do not reveal any *prima facie* signs of insanity. In a documentary, *A Question of Madness*, produced by Liza Key in 1998, Tsafendas was interviewed and comes across as normal. http://etd.uwc.ac.za/xmlui/bitstream/handle/11394/2912/Adams_PHD_2011.pdf?sequence=1
376 *Verslag, op.cit.*, 42.
377 *Ibid.*, 47.
378 J.A. Marais, *op.cit.*, 204.

International Court of Justice. The commission sat behind closed doors.[379] When B.J Vorster was criticised for this restriction on a matter of national concern and interest to everyone, he gave the feeble excuse that "I think that this matter is too serious".[380]

The enquiry was a complete whitewash. Although 105 witnesses were called, all the promising leads which might have exposed a conspiracy were either not initiated or simply abandoned.

(i) The journalist, Aida Parker, who wrote the sensational report in *The Sunday Tribune* on 28 August 1966 that 'Verwoerd must go' was not interviewed.[381]

(ii) The convicted communist attorney, Rowley Arenstein, who met Tsafendas on several occasions did not receive a *sub poena*.

(iii) The fact that Tsafendas visited the Greek ship, *Eleni*, while it was docked in Cape Town harbour for 40 days, almost every day, was not investigated to see if M-Apparatus, a secret group operating in a number of seamen's unions and connected directly with the Soviet Naval Espionage Service, was involved.[382] In October 1969 Mr. Patrick Walsh, Research Director of the Canadian Intelligence Service and a former under-cover agent of the Royal Canadian Mounted Police, "whose files on Communist movements and individuals are said to be second only to those in the possession of the RCMP",[383] visited South Africa and revealed that Tsafendas had long been a member of M-Apparatus.[384] This organization consisted of dedicated agents who concentrated on assignments such as courier work, naval espionage, political assassination, smuggling and getting prominent Reds out of countries when they were about to be jailed. Mr. Walsh had a close consultation for one and a half hours with General van den Bergh in Pretoria.[385]

(iv) The disclosure that four days before the assassination someone had asked an English politician, Allan E. Lomas, on 2 September 1966 in Dieppe, France, if there was any news of Dr. Verwoerd's death and that this enquiry was subsequently reported in the London, *Evening Standard* of 6 September 1966, received only cursory attention.[386]

---

379 *Ibid.*, 200.
380 *Ibid.*, 200.
381 *Ibid.*, 204. Shortly after her death in 2002, Aida Parker's office was raided by the Security Police and all her files were removed illegally.
382 J.J.J. Scholtz. *op.cit.*, 123-124.
383 I. Benson, Tsafendas – A Trial?, *Behind The News*, December 1969, 3.
384 I. Benson, File on Tsafendas, *Behind The News*, October 1969, 3.
385 I. Benson, Tsafendas – A Trial?, *Behind The News*, December 1969, 3-4.
386 J.A. Marais, *op.cit.*, 203-204.

(v) Dr. E. L. Fisher's eye witness statement[387] that Tsafendas must have been trained to wield a knife so professionally was ignored.

(vi) Christo von Malen, a carpenter from Pretoria, gave a sworn affidavit on 5 October 1966 to the SA Police that in November 1964 a motor car stopped next to him 100 yards from Libertas, Dr. Verwoerd's Pretoria residence. The driver of the vehicle was Denis Stefanus and one of his two passengers was Tsafendas. They asked von Malen if he could arrange entry into Libertas, but he said that it would be impossible. A few days later these three persons visited von Malen and asked him to help obtain a sketch of Libertas and showed him a pile of bank notes. Von Malen refused and then was attacked with a knife and had to be hospitalized. The Commission said that his allegations were improbable and dropped the matter.[388]

As may be observed from the above, Judge President Beyers and Judge van Wyk abused the rules of evidence and were, moreover, negligent, insouciant, if not downright dishonest in their application of the M'Naghten rules, where every man is presumed sane unless proved otherwise. Both justices brought the South African legal system into disrepute, and betrayed the public's trust in their so called "independence" with their egregious and amateurish attempts, seemingly, to protect the conspirators who were responsible for the murder of Dr. Verwoerd.

The Commission's Report, which exonerated both the Secretary and the Deputy Secretary of Parliament of having been guilty of any negligence, was tabled before parliament on 13 February 1967.[389] Both B.J. Vorster and Hendrik van den Bergh had been responsible for the security of Dr. Verwoerd and the parliamentary buildings. They were lambasted by the opposition United Party members of parliament for their gross incompetence and negligence. In his closing words, the member for Pinelands, Ossie Newton Thompson, said the following:

"Mr. Speaker, nothing less than [the resignation of the Ministers of Internal Affairs and Immigration and the previous Minister of Police, B.J. Vorster] will demonstrate the seriousness of the disclosures in this report and will indicate sufficiently that the government treats these disclosures in the same shocked manner in which the country also treats them. If the Cabinet and the members on the other side feel completely complacent, then it is just as shocking evidence of this decline in standards. In the old days in Japan people who leave their country in the lurch commit *hara-kiri*. In the Western world

---
387 *Ibid.*, 208.
388 Verslag, *op.cit.*, 74-76.
389 J.J.J. Scholtz. *op.cit.*, 142.

ministers hand in their resignations, and we are waiting to see that happen".[390]

Tsafendas was incarcerated at Pretoria Central and Zonderwater prisons for 28 years and spent the last five years of his life at Sterkfontein psychiatric hospital until his death on 7 October 1999. The question may be posed as to why Tsafendas was not released in 1994. The ANC are unlikely to have had any say in this matter, as their controllers would not have liked there to have been any unfavourable and embarrassing revelations, particularly as many of the participants in Dr. Verwoerd's murder – Oppenheimer, Rupert, Jacobson - were still alive and Tsafendas was *compos mentis* right until his end.

CUI BONO

The principal beneficiaries of Dr. Verwoerd's assassination were the International Money Power, and in particular the Rothschild bankers, although they would have to wait 28 years before they could collect their prize. Locally, Anton Rupert had *carte blanche* with which to expand his business empire as he desired, with far less hindrance from government interference. At Dr. Verwoerd's funeral held on 10 September 1966, Rupert was overheard by one of the mourners saying: *"Hoe lank sou ons hom nog kon verduur?"* (How much longer could we tolerate him). Later that month that negative disposition was repeated when he stated in Maseru, Lesotho that:

"I do not wish to be a hypocrite: the fact that Dr. Verwoerd was no longer Prime Minister was the best thing that could have happened to South Africa. Dr. Verwoerd was too stubborn and would not allow anyone to teach him how to rule a country. I had approached Dr. Verwoerd on numerous occasions to make apartheid more flexible, but Dr. Verwoerd did not take any notice".[391]

For Harry Oppenheimer, Dr. Verwoerd's demise brought about a great sense of relief. The recommendations of the *Hoek Report* would no longer be implemented and Anglo American could continue paying minimal tax and exploiting their black mineworkers. With his puppet, B.J. Vorster, in the premiership, he was strategically well placed to oversee the dismantling of apartheid and South Africa's incorporation into the plutocrats' New World Order. Mr. Oppenheimer[392] would live to see the realisation of his aim to have

---

390 J.A. Marais, *op.cit.*, 192.
391 *Ibid.*, 159-160.
392 One of the author's clients in the early 1980s, while he was working for a firm of stockbrokers in Johannesburg, was Harry Oppenheimer's former private secretary, Gerald Isemonger. He related the following anecdote. Once when he and Oppenheimer were travelling by train in Switzerland, a young man enquired as to what Harry Oppenheimer did for a living. He replied: "I work in the accounts department of Anglo American and De Beers".

Nelson Mandela inaugurated as the first black president of South Africa. Their friendship dated back to the early 1950s when he advised Mandela to spruce up his image by visiting his merchant tailor, Alfred Kahn in Commercial Street, Johannesburg. In 1994 it was reported that Harry Oppenheimer "likes Mr. Mandela very, very much",[393] while in *USA Today* of 20 June 1994, Oppenheimer boasted that he had been the "quiet engine that had powered the ANC".

It had taken 92 years to complete the journey back to Vereeniging[394] where on 31 May 1902 the Boers had been forced to give up their freedom at the end of the second Anglo-Boer War.

---

393 J.A. Marais, *The Founders of the New South Africa*, pamphlet, Pretoria, 15 July 1994, 27.
394 While he sat in the House of Assembly, F.W. de Klerk, who is considered by many people to have been a traitor, held the National Party seat of Vereeniging.

Chapter IX

CONCLUSION

At the time of his death, Dr. Verwoerd had reached the apogee of his powers, so too had South Africa reached a peak of prosperity which is unlikely to be achieved again. On numerous occasions Dr. Verwoerd predicted the fate that awaited South Africa if civilized rule were to be abandoned and replaced by a lawless and incompetent Black government under the suzerainty of the International Money Power.

On 9 March 1960 Dr. Verwoerd gave the following prescient warning in parliament to all the white nations of the world.

"May the white man, may the White nations of the world, also Britain, not lose their intellectual hold or in any other way. If they abdicate on our behalf and surrender, then in the long run the the flood of coloured people will not only overwhelm us, but in the years to come will reach their lands, and eventually overwhelm them too".[395]

On 12 December 1961 in a speech given to the Council for Coloured Affairs Dr. Verwoerd spoke as follows:

"What happens if the whites lose their hold on a unitary state? Who runs the country? Not the Coloureds, but the Bantu. I do not wish to insult the Bantu as a group, because I must also seek justice for them. The fact is that the experience in Africa proves that if the Bantu obtains authority over a country, it will lead necessarily to a dictatorship of a small group of politically interested parties amongst them. The Bantu masses will be subject to them and will perhaps suffer far more than the suffering that they are alleged to experience under a white government".

"As far as the other groups are concerned they will without a doubt be pushed backwards, perhaps quickly, perhaps step by step. The Coloureds should not think that they will be the last to be excluded from the rule of, participation in and benefits of such a mixed society. They can easily be the first. Which group will be respected the least by a Bantu dictatorship and be the least needed? Will it not be the Coloureds? The Whites' prestige and help might still be retained because of the usefulness of his knowledge".[396]

---
[395] *Verwoerd aan die Woord, op.cit.*, 346.
[396] *Ibid.*, 602-603.

In a speech celebrating the fifth anniversary of the Republic on 31 May 1966, Dr. Verwoerd said that:

> "As far as the Bantu are concerned will it be to their advantage if they become the dominant group, but in that process lose their separate national identities, and probably their languages and customs and suffer as a result of their incapacity – which we know is the case – to lead, manage and develop the phase of western civilisation which this country has reached in respect of industrialisation and other things?
>
> Would it be right in respect of their own masses? The few who obtain power might be satisfied, but for all we know they may be prodigals. For a large extent the masses would become unemployed and experience difficulty as we have seen in the rest of Africa. Would it be morally right to create the appearance of freedom, but in reality to cause living conditions similar to slavery".[397]

WHAT DOES THE FUTURE HOLD?

We have already observed an example of Dr. Verwoerd's forecasting skills, when he predicted that under Black majority rule, Rhodesia would disintegrate into chaos. In the above cited predictions, made over 50 years ago, we are able to bear witness to those events unravelling before our eyes – the unrelenting flood of millions of economic migrants into Europe, the blatant discrimination practised against Coloured people in their own homeland, the Western Cape, and the unabated suffering which the great majority of Black people now endure under Black rule.

In the last mentioned case we see that Black unemployment has risen from 5% to officially 26%. According to trade union COSATU it is 36%, but if one includes those who are no longer seeking work and those who are only partially employed, in other words subsisting, the figure rises to 50%. As a result of all this unemployment, 50% of the Black population lives below the poverty datum line with seven out of ten Black children living in poverty.[398] There are now 17.5 million recipients[399] of social grants out of an estimated population of 54 million. The rand which was worth $1.40 during the 1960s is now worth less than 6 US cents. From 1960-1966 South Africa was ranked as the 12th most developed country in the world, but has since lost that status and is currently classified as a developing country. During Dr. Verwoerd's premiership South Africa was a peaceful country with an almost total absence of serious crime.

---
397 Ibid., 677.
398 http://www.statssa.gov.za/publications/Report-03-10-06/Report-03-10-06March2014.pdf
399 https://nolstuijt.wordpress.com/category/sa-taxpayers-35-heavy-burden-17.5million-welfare-recipients-south-africa-economic-freedom-in-our-lifetime-campaign//

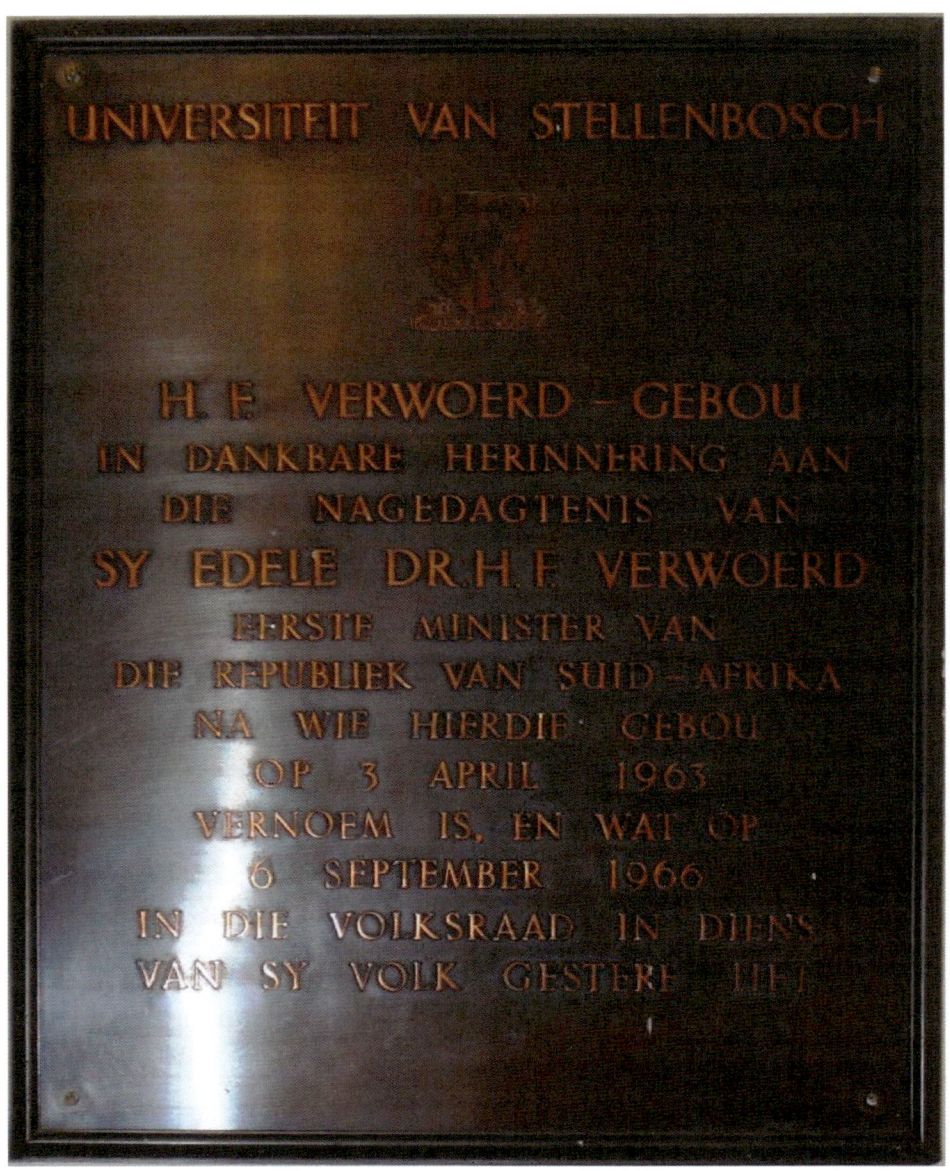

For three years the author attended lectures in economics at the H.F. Verwoerd building at the University of Stellenbosch. On 27 May 2015 the plaque in the foyer dedicated to Dr. Verwoerd was removed, without consulting the alumni, in an act of cultural vandalism. The author protested to the rector, Prof. Wim de Villiers, who replied in a letter that the plaque was "a symbol of institutionalised oppression and suffering" and that the objective of its removal was to create "a welcoming campus culture for all our students".

The annual murder rate was 60, whereas according to the *United Nations Statistical Year Book* since 1994 there has been an average of 20,000 murders per annum. An important litmus test is the Gini coefficient which statistically measures the distribution of income, and is used by both the United Nations and the Organization for Economic Cooperation and Development. A figure of 1 indicates that the entire income is held by one person, whereas 0 would mean that the inhabitants of a country would each have the same amount of income. In 1975 the co-efficient for Blacks was at the world average of .47.[400]

To-day South Africa has the worst co-efficient in the world at .70.[401] This dismal statistic is confirmed by the United Nations Human Development Index, which is a broader measure of welfare, and measures factors such as quality of life, life expectancy and progress in education. In 1995 South Africa occupied 59th position in the world at 0.741, whereas in 2014 it had dropped 47 places to 116th at 0.666.

What does the long term future hold? The Whites, who are the bearers of modern Western civilisation and the cement which has held South Africa together since its inception, are declining in numbers both absolutely and relatively. With a white female fertility rate of less than 1.5,[402] a recent prediction[403] that by 2030 the White population will constitute less than 2% of the total population is not inconceivable. If this current demographic trend is maintained, there will be hardly any White people living in South Africa by the year 2100, which will inevitably have disastrous consequences for the remaining population, as has already been observed in Zimbabwe.

What are the implications for the other races? With the future absence of the White farmers, who are currently being threatened with expropriation of 50% of their land without compensation,[404] and who feed the nation by providing 95% of all foodstuffs,[405] and the minerals of South Africa having been largely depleted, thus severely limiting the ability to import food – starvation will intensify and cause the other races to experience sharp declines in their numbers too. Such a dramatic fall in population would presumably be in line with the objective of the New World Order planners to reduce the world's population from its current 7.4 billion to 500 million.[406]

---

[400] Whiteford A.C. & Van Seventer D.E., South Africa's Changing Income Distribution in the 1990s, *Journal of Studies in Economics and Econometrics*, Vol. 24(3), 2000.
[401] http://repository.up.ac.za/bitstream/handle/2263/40181/Harmse_South_2013.pdf?sequence=1
[402] The 2011 census recorded a White female fertility rate of 1.6.
[403] The Year Ahead With Clem Sunter, South Africa's Youth Time Bomb, 12 February 2015. http://www.gunsite.co.za/forums/showthread.php?60660-SA-s-ticking-time-bomb
[404] http://www.farmersweekly.co.za/article.aspx?id=62176&h=Without-compromise,-SA-agriculture-has-no-future
[405] http://www.censorbugbear.org/farmitracker/reports/view/3514 and http://www.iol.co.za/business/news/farm-report-warns-of-serious-problems-1.1845285
[406] http://endoftheamericandream.com/archives/from-7-billion-people-to-500-million-people-the-sick-population-control-agenda-of-the-global-elite

Manufacturing, which is the foundation of any nation's prosperity, has declined from a peak share of Gross Domestic Product (GDP) of 24% in 1981 to 12 % of GDP in 2016. This alarming decline in manufacturing illustrates the deindustrialisation of the economy which has been taking place, and which has been exacerbated in no small measure by the 35% decline in labour productivity since Dr. Verwoerd's era.[407] It also inhibits any possibility of reducing unemployment. The permanent inability of the great majority of the population, which has an average IQ of 70, to maintain, let alone advance a civilisation, built by those with an average IQ of 100, and who are rapidly vanishing, will result in the near total collapse of the infrastructure and the economy by 2050 at the latest.

Not only have Dr. Verwoerd's predictions been proven to be correct, so too have his policies which, had they been pursued diligently, would have created a paradise for all the inhabitants of this corner of the world. The fact that Dr. Verwoerd was targeted for elimination by the International Money Power, provides further confirmatory evidence that he was working in the interests of the common man. Those liberals suffering from cecity, who still persist in accusing Dr Verwoerd of "oppression" of the Black people, find themselves driven to the extremities of the lunatic fringe.[408]

George Herold Calpin, a former editor of *The Natal Witness* and author of *At last we've got our country back*, characterised Dr. Verwoerd as follows:

"His personality alone was a recommendation: no one could listen to him without admiring his astonishing brilliance and his understanding of a subject. He had the intelligence of a computer: if he ever took a note onto the stage it was nothing more than a reminder by his wife to cut his hair. He was the sort of man who would attract dislike from some on account of the mathematical brilliance of his intellect: he did not have a high capacity to attract people to him through friendliness, sympathy and human understanding. Personally he was a charming man, in many respects wonderfully naïve, without pretence and not at all sophisticated".[409]

Dr. Verwoerd was a philanthropist,[410] who was accorded the highest eulogium

---

407 www.adcorp.co.za news pages. In calculating this number, Adcorp standardised 'the output-per-worker measure by the amount of capital used in the production process, which yields output per worker, per capital'.
408 There are three kinds of lunacy:
(i) lunacy at birth.
(ii) lunacy acquired as a result of infirmity or old age.
(iii) induced lunacy.
The last named category is the most prevalent and is acquired as a result of brainwashing. A good example is the Germans who have been indoctrinated into believing that they were exclusively responsible for starting both world wars.
409 J.A. Marais, *op.cit.*, 222.
410 It may be noted that at the one-sided Truth and Reconciliation Commission held in Cape Town from 1996-

by the Black people by being designated *Rapula*,[411] the rainmaker and bearer of the good things in life. He was also called *Sebeloke*,[412] the protector of the people.

Dr. Verwoerd is rivalled only by U.S. President John F. Kennedy, who was also murdered [413] by the international bankers on 22 November 1963 for trying to reform the Rothschild owned and controlled US Federal Reserve Bank,[414] as a worthy candidate for the accolade of having been the greatest statesman [415] of the world since World War II.

> 1998, not a single human rights abuse during Dr. Verwoerd's premiership was investigated, presumably because there were none. There was no enquiry about his assassination, notwithstanding the fact that both Tsafendas and Dr. Solly Jacobson were still alive, and that the latter was under police suspicion of having been involved in criminal activity.

411 F. Barnard, *op.cit.*, 46. Dr. Verwoerd received the moniker *Rapula* afer his first visit to South West Africa. Shortly after his departure heavy rains fell over many parched areas of the territory and he was immediately named *Rapula*. Many tribesmen carved wooden busts in honour of Dr. Verwoerd. C. Mutwa, *Indaba My Children: African Folktales,* Grove Press, New York, 1999, 657.

412 J.J.J. Scholtz. *op.cit.*, 80.

413 http://www.irishcentral.com/news/jackie-kennedy-blamed-lyndon-b-johnson-for-jfk-murder-127220093-237788131.html

414 Kennedy was also targeted because he refused to provide Israel with the components to make nuclear weapons and wished to terminate the Vietnam war. His assassins, firing from a grassy knoll as the motorcade went by in Elm Street, Dallas, were in all probability agents of the CIA/MOSSAD. According Dr. Arden Gifford, MD, who was a third year medical student and was present in the Emergency Room at Trauma Room 1 of the Parkland Memorial Hospital, Dallas, Kennedy had been stabilised, had good blood pressure and was about to be transferred to an Intensive Care Unit, where there was a possibility that he might recover from his ordeal. On the direct instruction of two secret service agents armed with 45 calibre revolvers, who were demanding the "body", Dr. William Kemp Clarke, Chief of Neurosurgery, removed the endo tracheal tube and all other life support, resulting in Kennedy's death within four minutes. Information provided to the author by Dr. Gifford. Kennedy's wife, Jackie, conscious of the potential danger to both herself and her son, fled to the sanctuary of a marriage with powerful Greek shipping magnate, Aristotle Onassis. See http://themillenniumreport.com/2016/03/jfk-jr-told-the-world-who-murdered-his-father-but-nobody-was-paying-attention-3/ which provides circumstantialevidence that CIA operative and later president of the United States, George HW Bush, was responsible for co-ordinating the murder. Kennedy's son, John F. Kennedy Jr., was aware of Bush's complicity and planned to expose him in his ironically named monthly magazine, *George*, but died in a mysterious airplane "crash" off the coast of Martha's Vineyard, Massachusetts on 16 July, 1999.

415 S.E.D. Brown, Verwoerd's Border Visit A Personal Triumph, *The South African Observer*, March 1961, 10. On the occasion of King William's Town celebrating the centenary of its foundation on 8 February 1861, Dr. Verwoerd "was given a warm reception by 4,000 Europeans and was also cheered and applauded by hundreds of non-Europeans". The Mayor, Mr. D.G. Galloway, described Dr. Verwoerd as "one of the greatest men in the world".

End Notes

1 In a speech given on 5 December 2015 to celebrate his 44 years on the Zulu throne, Goodwill Zwelithini kaBhekuzulu, King of the Zulus said that "The National Party had built a powerful government with the strongest economy and army on the continent, but then came this 'so called democracy' in which black people started destroying the gains of the past". http://www.iol.co.za/news/politics/king-praises-apartheid-regime-1.1956136#. VmVrVrh97cs See also http://www.telegraph.co.uk/news/uknews/1462042/Democracy-It-was-better-under-apartheid-says-Helen-Suzman.html 16 May 2004. Suzman said: "The poor in this country have not benefited at all from the ANC. The government spends money 'like a drunken sailor'. Instead of investing in projects to give people jobs, they spend millions buying weapons and private jets, and sending gifts to Haiti". P. Matjila, Black People Remembering the Past with Matchbox beats 'sim card' Once-despised township houses now preferred over RDPs, *Times Live*, 17 January 2011.

2 Speech given on 5 December 1950 to the Native Representative Council, Pretoria.

3 S.E.D. Brown, Apartheid In S.W.A. "Is Just", Chief Tells U.N., *The South African Observer*, April 1963, 11.

MAPS

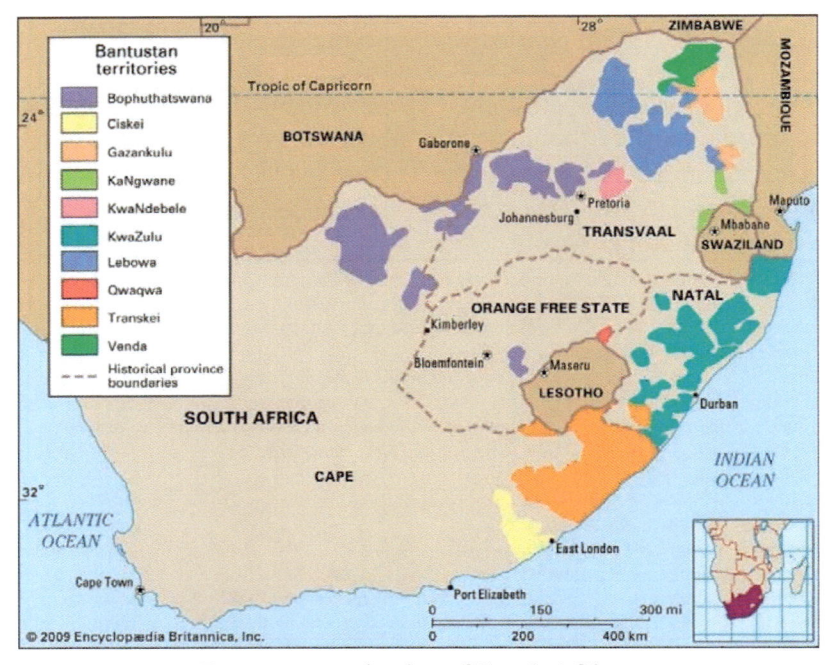

Bantustan territories of South Africa

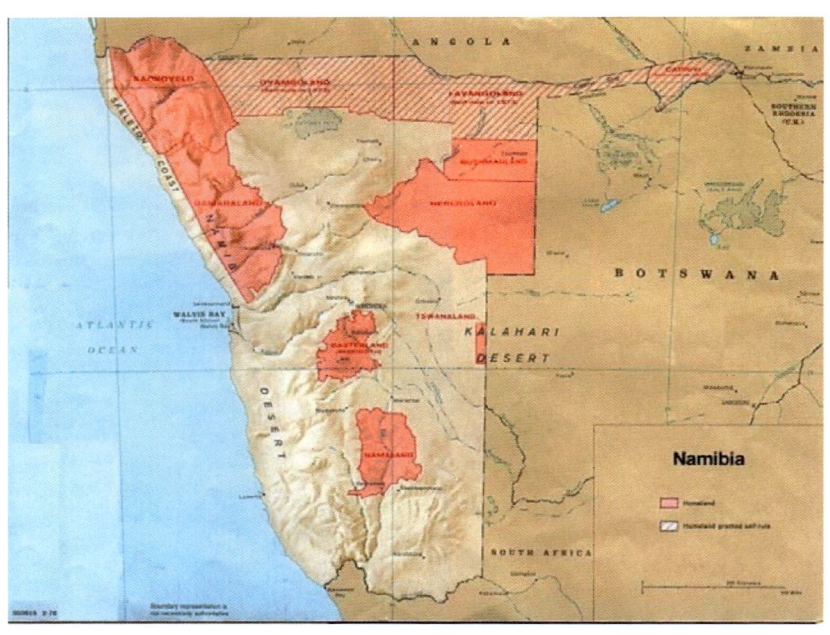

Homelands of South West Africa

Appendix I

Letter from Dr. H.F. Verwoerd to the author's grandfather, Mr. S.M. Goodson.

Kantoor van die Eerste Minister
Prime Minister's Office.

PRETORIA.

6th September, 1960.

Mr. S.M. Goodson,
"Mitford",
Rosmead Avenue,
KENILWORTH...Cape.

"MITFORD"
ROSMEAD AVENUE,
9 - SEP 1960
KENILWORTH, CAPE.

Dear Sir,

    I thank you for your letter of September 1st, 1960, with the suggestion that I should go down to Grahamstown to make an address on Settlers' Day. I fully appreciate the reason for your suggestion and would certainly have welcomed an occasion like this to demonstrate the genuine goodwill with which we are imbued towards our fellow-citizens. It would have been difficult, however, for me to address such an occasion unless invited to do so by those organising a festival on behalf of the Settlers. Particularly this year it would have been misunderstood if I made such arrangements myself, and perhaps even if there had been an invitation, since, it might be said that this was only a dodge to influence indirectly the voting on October 5th. Perhaps it will be better to remember this suggestion as a means of helping to consolidate our two population groups once the Republic has been brought about. It would then serve a double purpose, namely to demonstrate that we pay tribute without any ulterior motive and secondly to make clear that the history of the Republic of South Africa has roots in the history of the past of the English- as well as Afrikaans-speaking portions of our nation.
In other words, although you are right that a gesture now might be of value for objects we have in view for the immediate future, it may prove still more valuable at a somewhat later stage for the much more enduring objects we will then wish to serve.

Yours sincerely,

H.F. Verwoerd.

Appendix II

Dr. H.F. Verwoerd's Notes for his Speech on 6 September 1966

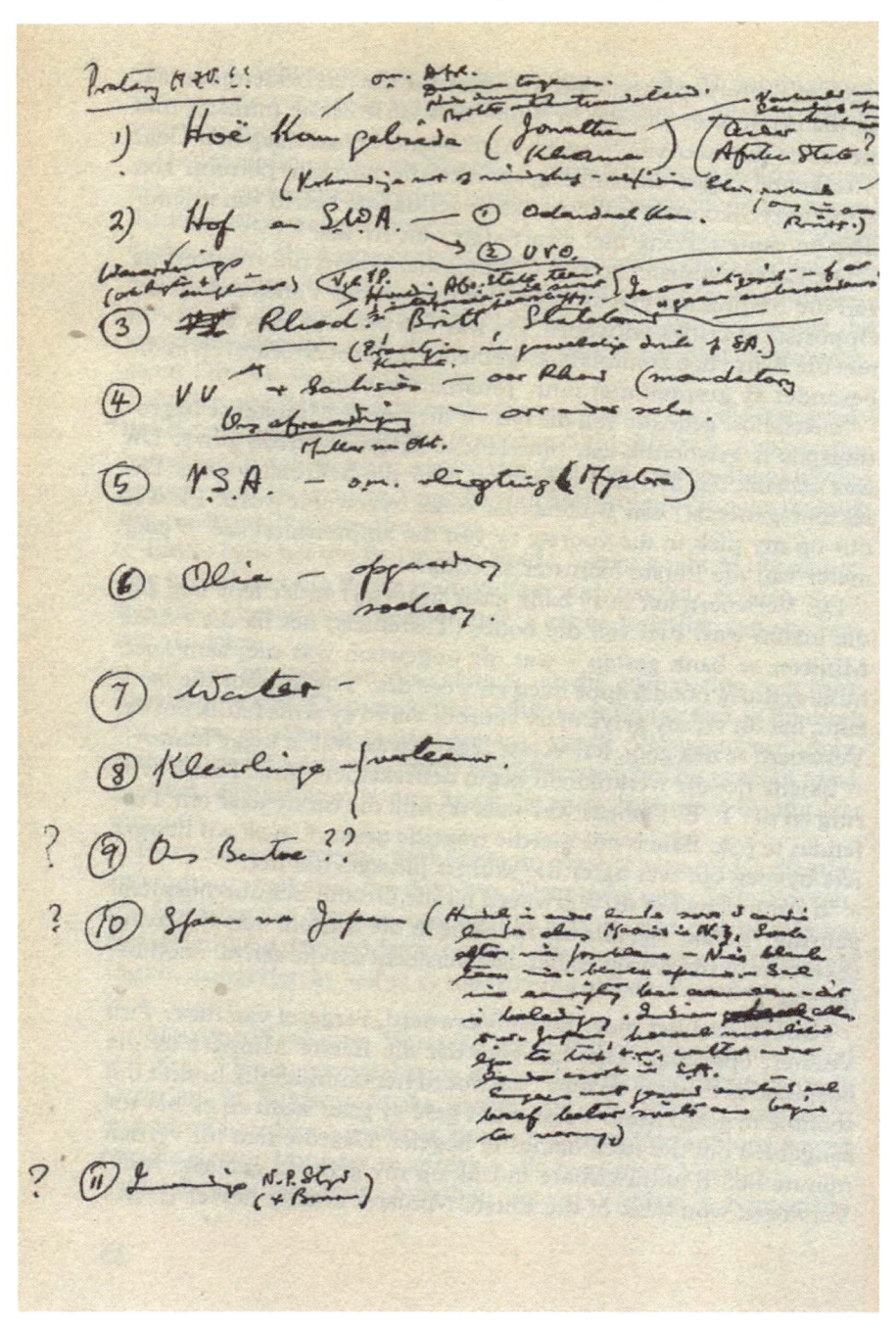

Deciphering of Dr. Verwoerd's Speech Notes of 6 September 1966 by Prof. W.J. Verwoerd

Ontsyfering van HFV se laaste toespraaknota vir 6.9.66
(Uit: Brandpunte, deur Brand Fourie, 1991, p. 54)
-------- is onduidelik

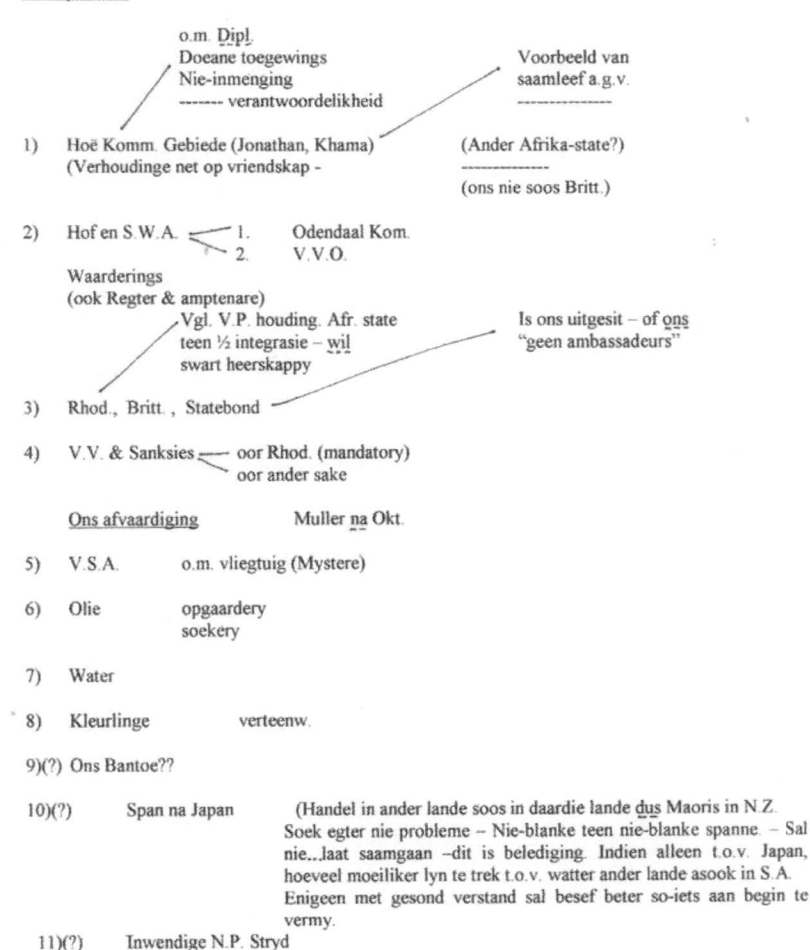

Pratery HFV!!

           o.m. Dipl.
           Doeane toegewings   Voorbeeld van
           Nie-inmenging   saamleef a.g.v.
           -------- verantwoordelikheid

1) Hoë Komm. Gebiede (Jonathan, Khama)   (Ander Afrika-state?)
    (Verhoudinge net op vriendskap -
                                            (ons nie soos Britt.)

2) Hof en S.W.A.   1. Odendaal Kom.
                  2. V.V.O.
    Waarderings
    (ook Regter & amptenare)
           Vgl. V.P. houding. Afr. state   Is ons uitgesit – of ons
           teen ½ integrasie – wil   "geen ambassadeurs"
           swart heerskappy

3) Rhod., Britt., Statebond

4) V.V. & Sanksies — oor Rhod. (mandatory)
                           oor ander sake

    Ons afvaardiging   Muller na Okt.

5) V.S.A.   o.m. vliegtuig (Mystere)

6) Olie   opgaardery
           soekery

7) Water

8) Kleurlinge   verteenw.

9)(?) Ons Bantoe??

10)(?)   Span na Japan   (Handel in ander lande soos in daardie lande dus Maoris in N.Z.
                                       Soek egter nie probleme – Nie-blanke teen nie-blanke spanne. – Sal
                                       nie...laat saamgaan –dit is belediging. Indien alleen t.o.v. Japan,
                                       hoeveel moeiliker lyn te trek t.o.v. watter ander lande asook in S.A.
                                       Enigeen met gesond verstand sal besef beter so-iets aan begin te
                                       vermy.

11)(?)   Inwendige N.P. Stryd
              (&Brown) Basson?

Appendix III

Letter from the leader of the Herstigte Nasionale Party, Mr. Jaap Marais, to the author.

Herstigte Nasionale Party

Pretoriusstraat 1043
Hatfield, Pretoria, 0083
Tel. (012) 342-3410

Posbus 1888
0001 Pretoria
Faks. (012) 342-3417

31 Oktober 1994

Mnr S M Goodson
Kilgettyweg 4
RONDEBOSCH
7700

Geagte mnr Goodson

Dankie vir u brief van 17 Oktober 1994 en die ingeslote afskrif van die betrokke brief en die weergawe in die Argus.

Ná die verskyning van die brosjure waarna u verwys, was daar 'n TV-uitsending oor dr Verwoerd waarin ek opgetree het. Baie onverwags het P W Botha my na aanleiding daarvan gebel. Hy sê toe onder andere dat binne 'n halfuur ná die sluipmoord John Vorster voor die aanvang van 'n buitengewone Kabinetsvergadering aan hom gesê het "This was a one man's job".

Natuurlik is dit 'n verstommende feit: die Minister van Justisie wat sonder enige ondersoek 'n ingrypende bevinding en uitspraak maak!

Ons oorweeg om die moord op dr Verwoerd en ander dinge wat nie die daglig kan verduur nie, by die sogenaamde Waarheidskommissie te opper — al is dit net ter wille van die geleentheid om dit weer in die openbaar te kry.

Met vriendelike groete

Jaap Marais

JAAP MARAIS
LEIER VAN DIE HNP

REVIEWS

Hendrik Frensch Verwoerd South Africa's Greatest Prime Minister, by Stephen Mitford Goodson, is a thoroughly referenced, cogent biography on the 'man of granite', whom I respectfully suggest remains immeasurably more than only South Africa's greatest Prime Minister', but is one of the greatest statesmen of our era.

Goodson's portrayal of Verwoerd is particularly valuable in going beyond the standard biographical details, and setting Verwoerd in historical context. Explained is the overwhelmingly distorted view of 'apartheid', which had been evolving in South Africa for three hundred years, and which Verwoerd made consistent and articulated as a philosophy of life. Only a few years ago Maori Party Member of Parliament, Dr. Pita Sharples could still get away on a TV interview with literally mistranslating 'apartheid as 'apart-hate'. In South Africa the policy was one of overwhelming success in the preservation and advancement of the myriad of separate identities and a doctrine of state that had the support of the majority of Blacks and Coloureds.

Studying sociology and psychology, Dr. Verwoerd was well aware of the complexities of human nature, including the distances between the racial psyches and cultures, 'ethnic psychology' being one of the subjects studied by Verwoerd in 1926. Entering politics in 1934, having been a professor of applied psychology, sociology and social science, Verwoerd's first interest was in dealing with the problems of poor whites. He served for several years as codirector of a social housing project in Cape Town. In 1936 he was appointed by Mr. W.A. Hofmeyr, Chairman of Voortrekkerpers, as editor of *Die Transvaler*. In 1938 he was elected to an executive position in the National Party. In 1948 he was elected to the Senate and in 1950 became Minister of Native Affairs, where he applied his scholarly expertise to learn about the Bantu and expected his staff to do likewise. From 1948, under the Nationalist Government, the laws were codified. This included the institution of identity papers, about which much nonsense has been written and spoken, designed to protect the employment of indigenous Africans in SA from the multitudes of Blacks who sought to migrate to SA for a better life under apartheid.

It was under Verwoerd that the generous allocation of land for self-administering homelands was instituted. Hospitals, schools, decent housing and sanitation were among the projects funded mostly from white taxes. Goodson provides the data for these achievements. Industries near, but not within the homelands, were encouraged. However, as Goodson shows, Oppenheimer and other plutocrats were intent on centralising industrial development within the cities, as a move to break down the homelands and necessitate Black migrant labour.

Nelson Mandela's mentor, Oppenheimer, always regarded the Blacks as primitive economic fodder.

In 1958 Verwoerd assumed the prime ministership of SA. Verwoerd was fully aware of who his enemies were, and exposed the Oppenheimer economic empire, and its global associations with the Rothschilds et al and homespun plutocrats led by Anton Rupert. The 'international money power', as Verwoerd called it, created a world campaign to vilify SA and bring down apartheid, so that, as Oppenheimer openly asserted, Black labour and consumption could be more fully utilised. Despite the impressive progress of SA economically, the plutocrats claimed that apartheid was stunting development, and it was Verwoerd specifically who had to go because of his stubbornness.

Plutocratic interests based in the USA played a major role in undermining SA, primarily through the *African Resistance Movement*. The Sharpeville Riot of 1960 was portrayed as a massacre of peaceful Blacks by White police, rather than as a murderous rampage by 20,000 machete welding Blacks converging on a police outpost. Not long after the Sharpeville riot, the first assassination attempt on Verwoerd's life was made by a demented multimillionaire, David Pratt.

In 1961 SA withdrew from the Commonwealth, as the campaign to isolate SA gained momentum in world forums such as the UN. Among those who opposed Verwoerd were the Israelis, who consistently voted against SA in the UN, despite SA's support for Jewish identity in Palestine. Verwoerd became fed up with the duplicity. (It could be added that this was a time when Israel had its own agenda of filling the power vacuum in Africa as the European colonial powers scuttled, hence their support for Idi Amin and for the Mau Mau for example).

The Rivonia Trial in 1963 provided added ammunition for the opponents of Verwoerd, when a terrorist Communist Party conspiracy had been unearthed.

One of the most interesting aspects of Goodson's book is the *Hoek Report* in 1964 by economics professor Piet Hoek, a study of the plutocrats, their association with international capital, and an ideological discussion of the anti-national character of capitalism. At the head of this was the Oppenheimer empire which was paying 5.4% tax on profits. Hoek recommended large-scale changes in dealing with these corporations, and state intervention in strategic assets controlled by the plutocracy. Verwoerd had already set SA on a path to self-sufficiency, and moreover, SA did not owe any debt to international finance.

In 1966 SA stood at the apex of its prosperity and progress. The plutocrats had been stating for years that 'Verwoerd had to go'. A rootless Coloured man, Michaelatos Tsafendakis, was chosen as the assassin. Goodson traces connections that involved in particular Anton Rupert, that implicate Johannes Vorster, Verwoerd's successor, CIA and MI6, among others. Goodson draws on the evidence of Dr. A. Bird, a SA neurologist, who had been a mentor to Dr. Solly Jacobson, a Communist Party functionary. Jacobson had associations with both Pratt and Tsafendakis, and it is suggested that both had been hypnotised and brainwashed by Jacobson. Tsafendakis, who took a job as a parliamentary messenger, despite a dubious past, was able to stab Verwoerd fatally, while Vorster stood by, shedding copious but unconvincing tears. Tsafendakis was declared insane and jailed for 28 years, after which he ended his last five years in a mental hospital. Vorster who was to succeed Verwoerd ensured that the hearing into Verwoerd's death was held in secret and in short order.

Vorster paved the way for the dismantling of apartheid by stealth, despite the hard man image by which he was portrayed. The Hoek recommendations were buried and the report stifled. Mandela delivered SA to the privatisation and globalisation that Oppenheimer, Rupert et al sought, but ironically, the Oppenheimer empire is, as Goodson shows, now a feeble shadow, while SA has predictably been reduced to an irredeemable shambles.

KERRY BOLTON PHD

Stephen Goodson's survey will astonish most English-speaking South Africans. The English Press and the four main English language universities painted Dr. Verwoerd as a petty racist. Even today, they remember him as the "architect of apartheid", by which they mean that racism was his first principle of government – the protection of white people and disrespect for the aspirations of black people.

Dr. Verwoerd's first principle of government, the author shows us, was that the highest levels of attainment in our society must be protected, so that those attainments can spread to others. Dr. Verwoerd warned that the Liberal principle of pretending that different levels of attainment were unimportant would destroy the quality of life in South Africa.

We see that he attended Milton High School in Bulawayo, and won many prizes, including one for the best pupil in English literature in all the schools of Rhodesia. His successes continued at Stellenbosch University, where he was among the leaders of the cultural life. He was awarded his degree *cum laude* and was offered a Sir Abe Bailey scholarship to study at Oxford, but preferred to study in Europe. Aged 26, he was appointed Professor of Applied Psychology, Sociology and Social Science. Dr. Verwoerd's talents were a gift for South Africa and it is an ominous sign, in these days of no leadership from South Africa's government, that his talents were so scorned.

Dr. Verwoerd started a federation of cantons, aka homelands, Swiss style, preserving languages and traditions, and offering evolution by mutual help. Stephen Goodson writes that the border industries remedied the separation of families, a crippling scourge that now afflicts most South Africans: "Bantu workers were able to commute daily to their place of work and live with their families, which was an important factor in promoting social stability. They were also able to spend a portion of their income in the homelands."

Why was Dr. Verwoerd's vision attacked in the Press and the universities of the country's most influential component, the White English-speaking South Africans? So thoroughly did the English language Press poison the minds of its readers against Dr. Verwoerd that no record can be found of his ever having spoken at an English language university.

It was the Money Power at work, says Stephen Goodson, whose special interest is banking. The "winds of change" were not intended to liberate the people of Africa, but to replace one form of control which was honest with another form of power exercised dishonestly through puppet regimes. "The colonial powers would save on the expense of having to subsidise and develop these colonies..., while the international bankers led by the Rothschild syndicate would plunge these hapless territories into irredeemable and permanent debt. They would be ably assisted by the economic hit men of the International Monetary Fund and World Bank."

The faculties of Political Science and Economics at Witwatersrand University, which ought to have tried to understand accurately the plans of their country's Prime Minister, were eclipsed by the Institute of International Relations, sited on the campus of Witwatersrand University in its own new building, "Jan Smuts House". The building was rightly named, as the author has shown us, after one who sold himself to the International Money Power and betrayed his people.

Dr. Verwoerd was an implacable foe of the Money Power, Stephen Goodson tells us, and wanted to achieve independence for South Africa. He commissioned the *Hoek Report* from Professor Piet Hoek of Pretoria University, and the report showed that the Anglo American Corporation controlled the English language newspapers and 70% of all companies in South Africa, while paying 10% of the tax.

The Anglo American Corporation also controlled the English language universities. Its Chief Executive, H.F. Oppenheimer, was chairman of the South African Institute of International Affairs, and his corporate subordinates occupied the Councils of the English language universities. Pretending to be an honest enterprise, the Institute promoted the interests of international corporations, and still does. The political message taught to the students was controlled by Oppenheimer and his associates.

Helen Suzman, the "lone voice in Parliament" of the Liberals, was in close communication with Harry Oppenheimer and both were counted as leaders in the English language universities. "Is Dr. Verwoerd sincere when he offers 13% of the land to 80% of the population?" Helen Suzman asked a hall full of laughing students at Witwatersrand university. "I am one of those who believes that Dr. Verwoerd is sincere. Oh don't get me wrong, a snake can be sincere."

The value of land is not measured by hectares. The author shows that Dr. Verwoerd's apportionment to the Bantustans was generous, and included the world's richest deposits of platinum. His desire was to have prosperous neighbours by being a provider of knowledge, service and aid. The living standard of Blacks was rising at 5,4% per year against that of the whites at 3,9% per year.

Dr. Verwoerd's Bantu Education was also ridiculed. How is education now, in the present unitary, multi-cultural state? The head of the Eastern Cape schools department, forced recently to supply evidence in a court case, has testified that his department is an utter failure, with no decision making capacity, no financial controls and unable to fill thousands of vacant posts for teachers. In another province, pupils received no text books, 5,000 of which were found dumped in an open field.

The author quotes a black academic, Rabelani Dagada at the Wits School of Business: "After twenty years of democracy, the education levels have plunged." Of black and coloured students enlarging the classes at university level, only 5% finish. Of the 1.1 million black children who were born in 1994 and later entered first grade, fewer than half made it to the final graduation exam. Of the moronic passing levels, the editor of South Africa's *Financial Mail* magazine, Barney Mthombothi, writes: "As long as pass mark is 30% ... we're fooling nobody but ourselves."

The standard of graduates from what were once the country's best universities is revealed by the collapsed state of essential services in this country. The national economy depends on electricity, and yet 33% of the capacity that existed in 1994 has been lost. Economic growth, between 6 to 8% under Dr. Verwoerd and the second highest in the world, is now 0.5%. In the rural areas, famine stalks the land. The murder rate, 60 per annum under Dr. Verwoerd, is over 20,000, twice that of the NATO war zone, Iraq.The author points to the collapse of government and unhindered plunderin that has been the result of "independence" in Africa. He shows us Dr. Verwoerd's belief that South Africa could do a far better and quicker job than Britain of leading the Bantu people to independence and economic prosperity, and that Verwoerd's opinion was shared by most South Africans. Chief Kaiser Matanzima, chairman of the Transkeian Territorial Authority, spoke to British television about racial conflict between Black and White in Britain, the United States and Southern Rhodesia, and he said that Dr. Verwoerd was "the greatest leader who has emerged among White South Africans". Dr. Verwoerd received a standing ovation for his speech given on 12 December 1961 to the Council for Coloured Affairs in Cape Town. On 16 May 1962, Dr. Verwoerd addressed five hundred mainly English speaking prominent business men and economists at the Wanderers Club in Johannesburg and again received a standing ovation.

Finding that support for Dr. Verwoerd was established and unshakeable among most South Africans, the international bankers resorted to bringing a case against South Africa in the International Court of Justice in The Hague, alleging that South Africa had failed to promote the interests of South West Africa's inhabitants. The case failed and, six weeks later, the bankers resorted to violence. In August 1966, the first terrorist attack took place on the northern border of South West Africa, and a month after that, Dr. Verwoerd was murdered.

The author describes a meeting at Harry Oppenheimer's Brenthurst estate in Parktown. The Minister of Justice, B.J Vorster, was asked to attend. "Also present were Anton Rupert, Quintin Whyte, a Council on Foreign Relations member and CIA agent, as well as an unknown representative of MI6. At this meeting, which lasted two and a half hours, a plot to assassinate Dr. Verwoerd was discussed." Vorster, a Freemason since his student days, was promised the premiership, conditional on his stealthily dismantling the apartheid structure and White leadership and handing over to designated Black puppets.

There were two attacks on Dr. Verwoerd's life, and both attackers were connected to the same sinister figures, with Oppenheimer as their principal. B.J. Vorster succeeded as Prime Minister, the *Hoek Report* was stifled, and the South African Defence Force was withdrawn from helping to defend gradualism in Rhodesia and began the infiltration and destruction of our two neighbours, Mozambique and Angola; all deeply significant historical factors that helped to neutralise White influence in Africa and usher in fundamentals there which are sought by the New World Order.

The choice in southern Africa was described at the time by an international lawyer, Anthony D'Amato, commenting on the South Africa case in The Hague: either to apply "pressure for reforming the system bloodlessly so that eventually the vastly more populous "Natives" will achieve political supremacy but the "Whites" remain an important, propertied, and perhaps respected segment of the citizenry", or "advocacy of immediate overthrow of 'White' supremacy, disregarding the safety of the 'Whites'".

Helen Suzman, supported by the Money Power on the Opposition side of Parliament, advocated immediate overthrow. On the Government side, Prime Minister B.J.Vorster, bribed by the money power, worked for the same end. In her autobiography, Helen Suzman tells that B.J. Vorster afterwards suggested to her that she had been used, and she concedes that he might have been right. In March 2016 the Helen Suzman Foundation was robbed of its computers at gunpoint, and the indications are that the instigators were members of the Government, wishing to eliminate evidence.

On the 5th December 2015, speaking to celebrate his forty-four years on the Zulu throne, King Goodwill Zwelethini kaBhekuzulu said, "The National Party had built a powerful government with the strongest economy and army on the continent, but then came this 'so-called democracy' in which black people started destroying the gains of the past."

With cultures and languages still whole, who knows what progress the now destitute rural areas might have made over the past sixty years? Looking northwards, we see the Mediterranean Sea dotted with refugees. The defences of European civic institutions are corrupted, and ancient centres of achievement are throwing themselves open to invasion by immigrants, levelling themselves down under the slogan, "There are no nations, only people". Stephen Goodson's examination of Dr. Verwoerd's leadership is more than South African history; it throws light on the same processes manipulating the rest of the world.

COLIN JACKSON BA (HONS) (WITWATERSRAND)

Addressing the Western World of the post-World War 2 era as we stumble through the second decade of the 21st century, there is one thesis which can safely be postulated without a risk of any reasonable denial:

Already only a shadow of its former self, Western Civilisation is currently en route to extinction...and whatever your stance towards the Third Reich, the fact remains that the destruction of Germany in the wake of World War 2 ultimately proved to be the first (and enabling) stage of this state of affairs.

What does this have to do with Dr. H.F. Verwoerd, sixth Premier of a country called "South Africa" on the southern tip of the African continent? Well, South Africa was an outpost of Western Civilisation which did not join on the road towards decline in the post-War era. To the contrary: Verwoerd rather led the country to an all-time height of its power. He refused to be drawn into the Game Plan for the Demise of the West – and ended up bleeding himself to death under the dagger of an assassin. His death was the first (and enabling) stage of getting South Africa on the same road towards extinction, plotted by other post-War Western countries.

The latter thesis, as an explanation of Dr. Verwoerd's death, is rejected outright in many circles, of course. It is a thesis requiring learning- and knowledge of applicable history – where "learning history" means to *seek and find the powers* acting as *causes* for those *effects* which we experience as historical *events*. Only an all-out fool would believe that the basic thrust of history is a series of unplanned coincidences.

Why is it essential that *all* of *us* "learn history" in this way? Because if you do not know the true facts of the past, you cannot understand the present, causing inability to shape your future. And that future will be shaped – by those "in the know", who will do so in their own interest; not in yours.

Unfortunately though, the *powers* acting as *causes* for those *effects* which we experience as historical *events*, are everything but readily recognisable. Falsifications, denials, fraud, hypocrisy, corruption and a host of other ills in the interests of the powerful - so typical of human nature and human action – all contribute to a massively distorted image of official- and mainstream "history". Not only that: Reliable sources are scarce, difficult to come by, or might even become non-existent in certain instances - people are not eager to document their transgressions; and mostly, witnesses go to the grave with the kind of knowledge which could seriously jeopardise themselves or their families if broadcasted to the world. Yet the ultimate tool of deceiving and misleading the public at large is, simply..."silence". Most people in the West are allowed to say what they want; but the mass media institutions decide what they would grant exposure to, and what they would not. They can pronounce the death sentence on any truth, simply by not conveying it to the world at large. It is, in the words of Oswald Spengler, a "terrifying censorship of concealment"; all the mightier since the masses constituting the consumers of the mass media industry are mostly oblivious, even regarding the very existence of such "censorship".

That is why a book like *Hendrik Frensch Verwoerd – South Africa's Greatest Prime Minister by Stephen Mitford Goodson* is not only commendable but actually imperative reading; not only in South Africa but also abroad. The text being 121 pages, it is a thorough summary rather than a "magnum opus" on the phenomenon "Verwoerd"; which is fortunate in the sense that such a book is invariably read by a larger circle of people than books which span 600 pages or more. It is compiled of nine sensibly-divided Chapters; each dealing with a specific phase in the life of Verwoerd and rounded off with a Conclusion. Although concise, the book provides ample facts and evidence of the onslaught on Western Civilisation with reference to Verwoerd and his era; it enhances an understanding of the present; thus contributes towards empowering its reader to shape the future – and it does so by passing the mass media's "censorship of concealment".

There can never be too many efforts in this regard; given the astonishing extent of lies, political disinformation and non-stop character assassination which followed the physical assassination of Dr. Verwoerd up to this day. **The real purpose of this slander continuously heaped on Dr. Verwoerd and his legacy does not concern Verwoerd himself in the first place – it is aimed at killing the Boer-Afrikaner drive for self-determination in our own day and time. Hence the immense importance of corrective material regarding Verwoerd such as this book by Mr. Goodson in terms of our future, even more than our past.**

In Chapter 2 titled "Academia", many facts are provided illustrating the sheer intellectual brilliance of the future Prime Minister. Chapter 3 ("Editor of *Die Transvaler*") sketches the critical role played by Verwoerd in the run up to the National Party's victory in the general election of 1948; and Chapter 4 ("Minister of Native Affairs") provides insight into the strategic measures taken by Verwoerd regarding racial affairs already before becoming Prime Minister. It also convincingly rebukes the integrationists' favourite and monotonously repeated labelling of Verwoerd as "architect of Apartheid"; by citing the quotes and policies of Southern African rulers (many of them British) aimed at racial segregation and which started centuries before Verwoerd was born. This Chapter also provides insightful corrections on the many myths about "Bantu Education". Chapter 5 (dealing with Verwoerd's term as Prime Minister) is rife again with the correction of falsification and myths and rendering true perspectives; such as those surrounding the Sharpeville shootings and the circumstances under which Verwoerd bid the British Commonwealth farewell. It also contains other very interesting information, such as the relations between Dr. Verwoerd and the British Field Marshal Montgomery.

It is in Chapter 6 ("The international money power") where the book reaches its zenith of identifying the real nature of the opposition against Dr. Verwoerd and Apartheid, the role players involved, their motives and their countermeasures. Pages 76 to 87 make for startling reading, even to the well-versed in South African history. To cite just one example: H.B. Thom, Chairman of the *Afrikaner Broederbond* from 1954 to 1960 was openly involved in Oppenheimer's "South African Foundation", set up in 1960 with the declared aim of "getting rid of Dr. Verwoerd". This fact alone already provides irrefutable evidence of a lethal cancer in the inner circles of the *Volk* – years before the assassination of Verwoerd. Chapters 7 ("Some general observations") and 8 ("Assassination") continue to cite numerous examples of circumstantial evidence as to the real history of the dissatisfaction with the actions of Dr. Verwoerd and, ultimately, the plot to murder him. And whereas circumstantial evidence is deemed sufficient to prove a certain point in Criminal Law (that is, if no other inference can be reasonably drawn), it should definitely also be enough in the realm of History.

If I dare raise one aspect which I found unfortunate, it is the quotes from a certain book which purports to forward "direct evidence", additional to all the circumstantial evidence, that Verwoerd had been murdered in the course of a conspiracy in which some of the *Volk's* leaders and senior officials played a key role. That book is "Volksverraad" by Adv. Piet Pretorius. Let me state frankly: I do not doubt that the erstwhile Minister of Justice, who also controlled the Police, B.J. (John) Vorster; the Head of the Security Police (General Hendrik van den Bergh) and *others had in fact been* involved in the murder of Dr. Verwoerd. In view of overwhelming circumstantial evidence – amply provided in the book under review - one cannot come to another conclusion. But the allegations made by Piet Pretorius as "direct evidence" in this regard, fail even a rudimentary test against a host of generally known facts.

In short, the allegations of Piet Pretorius boil down to the following: As a 20-year old law student at Stellenbosch University, Vorster was initiated into Freemasonry. Since 1937, he spent his university holidays in Pretoria, being trained as an undercover agent for eventual infiltration of the *Ossewa Brandwag*. In early 1942, the authorities performed a fake "arrest" on him, after which Vorster spent the next two years at Pretoria Central Prison and in the internment camp of Koffiefontein in the Free State. Throughout his incarceration, Vorster received food parcels and regular visits from Julius First, high-ranking leader in the Communist Party, father-in-law of Joe Slovo. In 1958, Ernie Malherbe (head of Military Intelligence in the Smuts government during- and after the Second World War) tipped off Harry Oppenheimer that one of his former agents - Vorster – who had been used to penetrate the *Ossewa Brandwag*, was now appointed a Deputy Minister. When Vorster was appointed Minister of Justice in 1961, he was introduced by Anton Rupert to Harry Oppenheimer. At this time Vorster was recruited by the CIA and promised the premiership at some future date.

Even a brief investigation of these allegations by Piet Pretorius, shoots them into tatters: He worked- and played as hard as his siblings on the family farm in the eastern Cape. His academic results were top of his class from the beginning- to the end of his school career; and he devoured reading material - especially newspapers - from a young age. Typical of Afrikaners in the region where he was born and raised (the *Stormberge* was the hotbed of Cape Rebels during the Anglo Boer War), Vorster's father was vehemently opposed to British Imperialism and to its apostles like Louis Botha and Jan Smuts. Upon hearing about the death of Louis Botha, Vorster senior was visibly satisfied and revelled: "Now our *volk* will come into its own right". There is no indication whatsoever that Vorster junior differed with his father on this issue; quite the contrary. John Vorster could not have spent his university holidays in Pretoria from 1937 ("being trained as an undercover agent for eventual infiltration of the *Ossewa Brandwag"*) simply because the *Ossewa Brandwag* (OB) did not exist during 1937; nor for almost the whole of the next year (which was Vorster's final year at university). In 1937, South Africa was governed by General J.B.M. Hertzog, and blissfully unaware that Smuts would ever again get another chance in the chair of the Prime Minister.

On campus, Vorster was one of the youth leaders of the "Purified National Party" of Dr. D.F. Malan which broke away from Hertzog in 1934. Double membership- or joint support of this Party and the *Ossewa Brandwag* (like in the case of John Vorster) was the rule rather than the exception; until the diverse views of the Party and the OB on various aspects (such as acceptance of the parliamentary democracy system) prompted a struggle for the "hearts and the minds" of their communal pool of supporters; an NP propaganda campaign against the OB; and eventually a prohibition by the Party on joint membership. In the wake of the latter development, Vorster was kicked out of the Party. After the Second World War broke out, Vorster got married and practised as a junior attorney in the eastern Cape; playing a leading role in the OB until his arrest in 1942. It is improbable – to say the least – that he would have left his newly-wed wife for almost two years and the dreary life in a corrugated iron hut at Koffiefontein, as part of some bizarre Security Police scheme. (If he was an "agent", he would have been worth infinitely more to Smuts whilst moving around the broader citizenry, than to languish amongst those who were already removed as potential dangers to the State). He was never incarcerated in Pretoria. He definitely never received "regular visits and food parcels", from the communist leader Julius First: No Koffiefontein inmate received "regular visits" from anybody and as the inmates basically lived within one another's personal space, any exception to this rule, or inexplicable absenteeism, would have been glaringly obvious.

If Vorster really was a Freemason for more than 20 years by 1958, Oppenheimer surely would never have had to be "tipped off" that he became a Deputy Minister. And if the CIA "promised Vorster the premiership at some later stage", it was quite an opportunistic promise to make at that stage (1961). As it turned out, the CIA would have had 6 days to influence a party caucus of more than a hundred members. (Prior to the murder, the topic of a successor for Dr. Verwoerd was hardly breached by caucus-members; it was widely accepted that Verwoerd would govern for years to come). Not that Vorster needed particular boosting since his introduction of security legislation especially prior to- and after the Rivonia trial: He stood head and shoulders above the other Cabinet Ministers who (with the exception of Dr. Albert Hertzog) were a remarkably mediocre lot at the time. And if Vorster really was chosen as Verwoerd's successor due to CIA-machinations, the CIA's liaison man in the NP caucus must have been none other than one Jaap Marais: HE was the caucus member who took the lead in getting Vorster elected as Premier, after the murder on Dr. Verwoerd…

Unfortunately, the aforesaid nonsense out of the pen of Piet Pretorius kills off the scientific credibility of his other "direct evidence" regarding the plot to kill Dr. Verwoerd (even though some of it could be labelled "probable"). But half a century down the line, we still await a direct source and a watertight exposure of Vorster's links with the CIA, MI6 and the International Money Power. Meanwhile the reasonable, objective and well-informed observer simply cannot believe that those links did not exist; already due to the glaring improbability of the official version on some crucial aspects: The circumstances surrounding Tsafendas' work- and residence in South Africa at the time; the Vorster/Van den Bergh *modus operandi* after the murder; the fact that the Minister and his most senior official contradicted each other in media releases; the fact that Tsafendas skipped the scrutiny of a criminal trial under dubious circumstances, just like his predecessor Pratt; the fate of the "Hoek Report" after the assassination… to name but a few aspects. Dozens of hard facts like these relentlessly point towards a Vorster-Van den Bergh complicity and also to the conclusion that their actions must have been prompted by Powers behind the scene: Vorster did not have to murder Verwoerd solely to become Prime Minister. He would have taken over eventually in any event. With personal ambition ruled out as a motive for the killing, we are left with the alternative: The elimination of Verwoerd and the destruction of his work. Thus the central thesis in Mr. Goodson's book is saved, despite the quotes from Piet Pretorius.

Those who want to understand the present and be empowered to shape the future, should read this work of Mr. Goodson and, in fact, his other books as well. You cannot fight for survival, if you do not know who the enemy is.

Paul Kruger BA (Pretoria), BA (Hons) (UNISA), B Proc (Pretoria)

Bibliography

- H.R. Abercrombie, *The Secret History of South Africa or Sixty five Years in the Transvaal*, Central News Agency Ltd, Johannesburg, 1952.
- G. Allighan, *Verwoerd-The End*, Purnell & Sons (S.A.) (Pty.) Ltd, Johannesburg, 1961.
- F. Barnard, *13 Jaar In Die Skadu Van Dr H.F. Verwoerd*, Voortrekkerpers, Johannesburg, 1967.
- J. R. Baker, *Race*, Oxford University Press, 1974.
- G. C. Basson and N.F. Hefer, *Hendrik Frensch Verwoerd, pictorial biography*, Voortrekkerpers, Johannesburg, 1966.
- J. Basson, *"Meneer die Speaker!" Uit die Politieke Plakboek van Japie Basson*, Politika, Kaapstad, 2012.
- I. Benson, *Truth Out Of Africa Lessons for all Nations*, Veritas Publishing Company (Pty) Ltd, Cranbrook, Western Australia, 1995.
- A. Bird, *Bird on the wing: Autobiography, 1916-1992*, South African Natural History Publications, Johannesburg, 1992.
- A. Boshoff, *Sekretaresse Vir Die Verwoerds*, Human & Rousseau, Kaapstad, 1974.
- J. Botha, *Verwoerd is Dead*, Books of Africa, (Pty.) Ltd, Cape Town, 1967.
- L. J. Bothma, *Rebelspoor*, Self-published, Langenhovenpark, Orange Free State, 2015.
- M. Brokensha and R. Knowles, *The Fourth of July Raids*, Simondium Publishers, Cape Town, 1965.
- B. Bunting, *The Rise of the South African Reich*, Penguin Books Ltd, London, 1969.
- A.A. Cooper, *The Freemasons of South Africa*, Human & Rousseau, Cape Town, 1986.
- E. Dommisse, *Anton Rupert*, Tafelberg Publishers, Cape Town, 2005.
- G. Frankel, *Rivonia's Children: Three Families and the Cost of Conscience in White South Africa*, Jacana Media, Johannesburg, 2011.
- P.W. Grobbelaar, *Man van die Volk*, Human & Rousseau, Kaapstad, 1967.
- W.C. Halstead, *Brains and Intelligence: A Qualitative Study of the Frontal Lobes*, University of Chicago, 1947.
- A. Hertzog, *Waarheen Suid-Afrika? Oproep tot die Stryd*, Mrs M.M. Hertzog, Pretoria, sine dato.
- A. Hocking, *Oppenheimer & Son*, McGraw-Hill, Johannesburg, 1973, 353.
- *Hoek Verslag van Prof. Piet Hoek aan Dr H.F. Verwoerd*, 1965.

- H. Kenney, *Architect of Apartheid: H.F. Verwoerd An Appraisal*, Jonathan Ball (Pty) Ltd, Johannesburg, 1980.
- G. Ludi and B. Grobbelaar, *The Amazing Mr Fischer*, Nasionale Boekhandel, Cape Town, 1966.
- J.A. Marais, *Die era van Verwoerd*, Aktuele Publikasies, Pretoria, 1992.
- J.A. Marais, *The Founder of the New South Africa*, pamphlet, Pretoria, 1994.
- C. Marx, *Hendrik Verwoerd and the Leipzig School of Psychology in 1926*, Historia, vol. 58, no. 2, January 2013.
- B.L. Montgomery, *The Memoirs of Field-Marshal Montgomery*, Collins, London, 1958.
- D. Pallister, S. Stewart, I. Lepper, *South Africa, Inc.: The Oppenheimer Empire*, Yale University Press, New Haven, Connecticut, 1988.
- M. Pos, *Wie was Dr Verwoerd?*, De Banier, Utrecht, 1968.
- P.J. Pretorius, *Volksverraad*, Libanon-Uitgewers, Mosselbaai, 1996.
- C. Putnam, *Race and Reality*, Howard Allen Printing, Cape Canaveral, 1980.
- E. Ray, W. Schaap, K. van Meter, L. Wolf, *Dirty Work 2: The CIA in Africa*, Zed Press, London, 1980.
- B.M. Schoeman, *Die Broederbond in die Afrikaner-politiek*, Aktuele Publikasies, Pretoria, 1982.
- B.M. Schoeman, *Die Geldmag Suid-Afrika se onsigbare regering*, Aktuele Publikasies, Pretoria, 1980.
- G.D. Scholtz, *Dr Hendrik Frensch Verwoerd 1901-1966, Vols., 1 and 2*, Perskor, Johannesburg, 1974.
- J.J.J. Scholtz, *Die Moord Op Dr. Verwoerd*, Nasionale Boekhandel Bpk, Kaapstad, 1967.
- T.M. Silver, *Lifting The Veil An Investigative History of the United States Pathocracy*, http://www.wanttoknow.info/mk/liftingtheveil#5
- A. Sparks, *The Mind of South Africa, The Story of the Rise and Fall of Apartheid*, William Heinemann Ltd, London, 1994.
- P.C. Swanepoel, *Really Inside BOSS A Tale of South Africa's late Intelligence Service (And Something about the CIA)*, Self-published, Pretoria, 2008.
- H. Suzman, *In No Uncertain Terms*, Jonathan Ball Publishers, Johannesburg, 1993.
- B. Temkin, *Buthelezi A Biography*, Frank Cass & Co. Ltd, London, 2003.
- D.H. Thomson, *The Story Of A School A Short History of the Wynberg*

Boys' High School, Wynberg, Cape, 1961.
- M. van Bart, *Kaap Van Slawe*, Historical Media cc, Tokai, South Africa, 2012.
- *Verslag van die Kommissie van Ondersoek na die Dood van wyle Sy Edele dr. Hendrik Frensch Verwoerd,* Bienedell Uitgewers, Pretoria, 2000.
- *Hendrik Frensch Verwoerd Pictorial Biography 1901-1966,* Voortrekkerpers, 1966.
- H.F. Verwoerd, A Method for the Experimental Production of Emotions, *The American Journal of Psychology.* Vol.37, University of Illinois Press, July 1936.
- H.F. Verwoerd, *Loskopdamtoespraak,* Bienedell Uitgewers, Pretoria, 2000.
- *Verwoerd aan die Woord,* edited by Prof. A.N. Pelser, Afrikaanse-Pers Boekhandel, Johannesburg, 1966.
- *Verwoerd só onthou ons hom,* compiled by Wilhelm J. Verwoerd, Protea Boekhuis, Pretoria, 2001.
- J.D. Vorster and F.N. van Niekerk, *Die Vrymesselary Ontmasker,* Nasionale Boekdrukkery Beperk, Kaapstad, 1973.
- I. Wilkins and H. Strydom, *The Super-Afrikaners-Inside the Afrikaner Broederbond,* Jonathan Ball Publishers, Johannesburg, 1979.

Index

A

African American Institute 43
African National Congress 60, 61, 107
Afrikaanse Handelsinstituut 45, 74
Afrikaanse Pers Beperk 86
American Field Service 68
Anglo American Corporation 10, 11, 73-74, 77-82, 106
Anglo-Boer War 13, 105
Arden-Clarke, Sir Charles 57
Arenstein, Rowley Israel 95, 104
Association of Chambers of Commerce 45
Atlas Aircraft Corporation 75

B

Baasskap 37
Balewa, Sir Abubakr Tafawa 48
Baird, John Logie 69
Baird, Margaret 69
Ballinger, Margaret 45
Banks Act 79-80
Bantu Authorities Act 31
Bantu Education Act, 34
Bantu Investment Corporation 31, 80
Bantu Services Levy Act 30
Barnard, Fred 41
Benson, Ivor 74
Bernstein, Lionel 60
Beyers, Judge President Andries 102, 105
Bird, Dr. Allan 46-47, 94, 99
Bloomberg, David 102
Boas, Franz Uri 33
Botha, Louis 24, 54-55
Botha, Pik 59
Botha, P.W. 101
Bothma, Dr. Louis 10-11
Brink, Major General George 58
British Commonwealth 38, 41, 83
Broederbond 64
Brown, S.E.D. 72, 76

C

Caledon, Earl of 22
Calpin, George Herold 112
Canadian Intelligence Service 104
Carnegie Endowment for International Peace 59
Carpio, Dr. Vittorio 57
Central Intelligence Agency 39, 43-44, 58, 60, 78, 91, 93, 96, 100
Cillié, Piet 99
Chamber of Mines 45
Chuene, Chief 40
Coetzee, Brigadier Johan 94
Coetzer, W.B. 72
Coloured Persons Representative Council Act 32
Commission for the Socio-Economic Development of the Bantu Areas 29
Commission of Enquiry into the Circumstances of the Death of the late the Honourable Dr. Hendrik Frensch Verwoerd 103
Commonwealth Conference 47-49
Convention for the Promotion of Export Trade 70
COSATU 109
Council for Coloured Affairs 32, 108
Council for German Jewry 18
Council on Foreign Relations 59, 68, 91, 93, 96

D

Daniels, Helen 96
Dawson, Lieutenant Colonel F.S. 55
De Alva, Dr. Salvador Martinez 57
Degenaar, Prof. Johan 99
De Guigand, Major General Francis 51, 72
De Klerk, F.W. 9
De Klerk, Marike 10
De Villiers, Advocate David 59, 68
De Wet, Dr. Quartus 62
Diefenbaker, Prime Minister John 48
Dönges, Dr. T.E. 37
Duncan, Sir Patrick 26
Dutch East India Company 32
Du Toit, Hennie 86

E

East, A.S.A. 53
Economic Council of Advisers 70

Eksteen, Rian 59
Eleni 104
Emakuzeni 69
Eskom 70

F

Federale Mynbou Bpk 75
Festenstein, Hilliard 60
Fischer, Advocate Bram 61
Fisher, Dr. Ephraim 101
Forster, Richard 56
Fort Hare College 34, 36
Foskor 70
Franke, General Victor 55
First, Julius 91

G

General Mining and Finance Corporation Ltd 75
Gesuiwerde Nasionale Party 18
Gilbert, Prof. 88
Gini coefficient 111
Goldberg, Denis 60
Goldreich, Arthur 60, 62
Good Hope Model Housing Scheme 18
Graaff, Sir de Villiers 63
Gross, Advocate Ernest 59
Group Areas Act 31-32

H

The Hague Peace Conference 9
Hammarskjöld, Dag 50-51
Hepple, Bob 60
Herstigte Nasionale Party 80
Hertzog, J.B.M. 18, 30
Hoek, Prof. Piet 77-82
Hoek Report 10-11, 77-82, 106
Hofi, General Yitzhak 94
Hofmeyr, W.A. 19
Holyoake, Prime Minister Keith 48
Hottentot Code 22

I

Immorality Act 27
International Court of Justice 57, 104
International Monetary Fund 39
Iscor 10, 70, 77

J

Jacobson, Dr. Solly 46-47, 93-94, 106
Jansen, Dr. E.G. 22
Jensen, Prof. Arthur Robert 34
Joint Matriculation Board 35
Jonathan, Chief Leabua 89
Jooste, Marius 86

K

Kahn, Alfred 107
Kantor, James 60
Kathrada, Ahmed 60
Kennedy, John F. 113
Kenyatta, Jomo 62
Klem, Prof. Otto 16
Kossew, Dr. Ralph 102
Kissinger, Henry 96
Kruger, Prof. Felix 16
Kruger, President S.J.P 7-9, 11
Kruger National Park 70
Kutako, Hosea 56

L

Lagden, Sir Godfrey Yeatman 22
Landman, W.A. 99
League of Nations 55, 57
Leipzig Institute of Experimental Psychology 16
Leonhardt, Carl 97
Leonhardt, Joan 97
Le Roux, P.M.K. 96
Lidman, Sara 51
Lincoln, Abraham 8
London Convention 22
Louw, Eric 47, 53

Louw, Dr. M.S. 72
Lugard, The Lord 26
Lukin, Brigadier General Tim 54
Lutheran Primary School 13

M

Macmillan, Dorothy 40
Macmillan, Prime Minister Harold 40-42
Mackay, Prof. Vernon 58
Maisels, Advocate Israel 46
Malan, Dr. D.F. 18, 20
Malay Quarter 32
Malherbe, Colonel Ernie 90
Malherbe, Prof. W.M.R. 90
Mandela, Nelson 9, 46, 61-62, 107
M-Apparatus 100, 104
Marais, Jaap 46, 68, 102
Marais, Jan S. 72, 99
Maserumule, Chief Frank 40
Matanzima, Chief Kaiser 54
Maud, Sir John 43
Mbeki, Govan 60
Medical University of South Africa 36
Mental Disorders Act 47, 103
Menzies, Prime Minister Robert 48
Mhlaba, Raymond 60
Milner, Lord Alfred 22
Milton High School 14
MI6 39, 46, 91, 93, 96, 100
MK-Ultra 93, 100
Mlangeni, Andrew 60
M'Naghten rules 104
Montgomery, Field Marshal Bernard 51-52
Mossad 94
Motsoaledi, Elias 60
Muller, Tom 75
Mungunda, Aaron 56

N

Nathan, Justice Manfred 7-9
National Indian Council 32
National Intelligence Service 44
National Party 11, 19, 21, 23, 27, 32, 37, 45, 53, 72-73, 99

Native Abolition of Passes and Co-ordination of Documents Act 29
Natives Lands Act 23, 26
Native Laws Amendment Act 29
Native Trust and Land Act 30
Newton Thompson, Ossie 105
New World Order 68, 74, 89, 106, 111
Nobel Peace Prize 9-10
Nthite, Peter 51
Nkrumah, Kwame 48
Nujoma, Sam 56

O

Odendaal Commission 58
Odendaal, Frans Hendrik 58
Olivier, Prof. Nic 99
Olivier, Willie 101
Oppenheimer, Sir Ernest 55
Oppenheimer, H.F. 11, 72-75, 77-82, 89-91, 100, 106-107
Operation Mayibuye 60
Orange River Scheme 70
Organization for Economic Cooperation and Development 111
Ossewa Brandwag 20-21, 90-91

P

Pan African Congress 43
Parker, Aida 99, 105
Pienaar, Schalk 99
Pratt, David Beresford 45-47, 93
Pretorius, Advocate Piet 43-44, 93, 95
Progressive Party 53, 101
Prohibition of Mixed Marriages Act 27
Promotion of Bantu Self-government Act 38

R

Rapula 113
Reeves, Bishop Ambrose 43
Referendum 38-39
Rembrandt Tobacco 72
Rhodes, C.J. 7
Rhodesia and Nyasaland, Federation of 65
Richter, Colonel Carl 89
Robinson, Sir Hercules 22

Rockefeller, Nelson 96
Rothmans International 93, 97
Rothschild banking/dynasty/group 39, 55, 77, 89-90, 93, 99-100, 106-107, 113
Royal Canadian Mounted Police 104
Rupert, Dr. Anton 11, 19, 68, 72, 91, 93, 97, 99-100, 106

S

Sakinofsky, Dr. Isaac 102
Sasol 70
Schoombie, Betsie 16
Schumann, Dr. F.E.W. 68
Sebeloke 113
Security Council of the United Nations 44
Separate Amenities Act 31
Separate Development 27-29
Shapeka, Ananias 56
Sharpeville 11, 43-44, 68, 78
Shepstone, Sir Theophilus 26
Simon's Town Naval Agreement 63
Simon van der Stel Foundation 69
Slovo, Joe 46, 91
Smuts, Jan 20, 24-25, 34, 54-55, 90
Sons of England 64
South Africa Club 27
South African Broadcasting Corporation 69, 97
South African Communist Party 46, 91, 92
South African Federated Chamber of Industries 45
South Africa Foundation 72-74
South African Indian Council 33
South African Jewish Board of Deputies 53
South African Native Affairs Commission 22
South African Reserve Bank 82
Soviet Naval Espionage Service 101, 104
Spender, Sir Percy 59
S.S. Karanja 95
Stefanus, Denis 105
Stormjaer 21
Strydom, J.G. 21, 37, 75
Stuttgart 18
Swart, C.R. 9, 37, 84
Suzman, Helen 101

T

Thom, Prof. H.B. 68, 72
Thomas, Allan 104
Tomlinson Commission 29
Tomlinson, Prof. F.R. 29
Transvaal Roads Department 70
Tsafendas, Demetrio Mimikos 92-97, 99-106
Tsafendas, Michaelatos 92
Traill-Smith, Moyna 82

U

Umkhonto we Sizwe 60
Unilateral Declaration of Independence 66
Union Exposition 45
Union Festival 45
Unionist Party 26
United Nations 55-57, 88, 111
United Nations Human Development Index 111
United Party 11, 30, 37, 72-73
United South Africa Trust Fund 72
United States Federal Reserve Bank 113
United States Navy 64-65
United States South Africa Leaders Exchange Program 67-68
University of Bophuthatswana 36
University of Durban-Westville 36
University of Leiden 90
University of the North 36
University of Pretoria 77
University of Stellenbosch 15-17, 90
University of Venda 36
University of the Western Cape 36
University of Zululand 36
USS Independence 64

V

Van Bart, Marthinus 7
Van den Bergh, General Hendrik 80, 92, 94, 96, 102, 104-106
Van der Stel, Simon 22
Van Eck, Dr. H.J. 68, 72
Van Rensburg, Johannes Fredrik Janse 20
Van Wyk, Justice Theo 103
Versailles, Peace Conference 55

Verwoerd, Anje 13
Verwoerd, Dr. H.F. 7-11, 13-22, 24, 27-35, 37-54, 56-57, 59, 62-77, 80-89, 91, 93-106, 108-110, 112-113
Verwoerd, Leendert 13
Verwoerd, Hendrika 13
Verwoerd, Wilhelmus Johannes 13
Visser, Dr. Willie 103
Vista University 36
Volket, Prof. Hans 16
Von Malen, Christo 105
Voortrekkerpers 19, 86
Vorster, B.J. 10-11, 20, 82-83, 91-92, 95, 97, 100-102, 104-105

W

Wales, Prince of 21
Walsh, Patrick 104
Wassenaar, Dr. A.D. 99
Whyte, Quintin 91
Wilcocks, Prof. R.W. 15
Wilson, Harold 63
Winter, Gordon 47
Wolman, Judy 82
Wolpe, Harold 60, 62
World Bank 39
Wynberg Boys Junior School 13

Y

Yutar, Dr. Percy 60

Z

Zabow, Dr. Abraham 102

Printed in Great Britain
by Amazon